NEW VANGUARD 330

# BRITISH LEND-LEASE WARSHIPS 1940–45

The Royal Navy's American-built destroyers and frigates

**ANGUS KONSTAM**          ILLUSTRATED BY ADAM TOOBY

OSPREY PUBLISHING
Bloomsbury Publishing Plc
Kemp House, Chawley Park, Cumnor Hill, Oxford OX2 9PH, UK
29 Earlsfort Terrace, Dublin 2, Ireland
1385 Broadway, 5th Floor, New York, NY 10018, USA
E-mail: info@ospreypublishing.com
**www.ospreypublishing.com**

OSPREY is a trademark of Osprey Publishing Ltd

First published in Great Britain in 2024

A catalogue record for this book is available from the British Library.

ISBN: PB 9781472861283; eBook 9781472861252;
ePDF 9781472861269; XML 9781472861276

24 25 26 27 28 10 9 8 7 6 5 4 3 2 1

Index by Alison Worthington
Typeset by PDQ Digital Media Solutions, Bungay, UK
Printed and bound in India by Replika Press Private Ltd.

Osprey Publishing supports the Woodland Trust, the UK's leading woodland
conservation charity.

To find out more about our authors and books visit
**www.ospreypublishing.com**. Here you will find extracts, author
interviews, details of forthcoming events and the option to sign up for our
newsletter.

Title page caption: A rare colour photograph of a 'four-stack' Lend-Lease
destroyer in British service, at the head of an Atlantic convoy, in mid-1941.
This is almost certainly a posed shot, with the crew of her starboard
midships 4in gun closed up at action stations.

# CONTENTS

# BRITISH LEND-LEASE WARSHIPS 1940–45

## The Royal Navy's American-built destroyers and frigates

### INTRODUCTION

On 3 September 1939, as a result of the German invasion of Poland, Britain and France found themselves at war. That evening, out in this crucial fight, the British liner SS *Athenia* was torpedoed by a German U-boat. It became the first casualty in the longest-running campaign of the war – the Battle of the Atlantic. At stake in this titanic struggle was Britain's very survival. The island-nation relied on the import of food and raw materials to survive. Put simply, if her maritime supply lines could be cut, then Britain would be forced to surrender. The British quickly organized their merchant shipping into convoys, but they lacked the escort vessels needed to properly protect them against growing numbers of German U-boats. Britain had the largest merchant fleet in the world, but losses mounted steadily, until it reached the point where ships were being sunk faster than they could be replaced. This is where the Battle of the Atlantic became a fight for survival.

When the war began, the British Admiralty initiated an emergency shipbuilding programme, but it would take time for these new warships to be completed. Meanwhile, after the fall of France in May 1940, the bulk of Germany's ocean-going U-boats were relocated to France's Atlantic coast, giving the boats easy access to their Atlantic hunting grounds. As a result, Prime Minister Churchill asked President Roosevelt for 'the loan of forty or fifty of your oldest destroyers to bridge the gap' until newly built escorts could enter service. So, a deal was hatched where British overseas bases would be transferred to the United States in exchange for some of these obsolete 'four-stack' destroyers.

An initial batch of 16 warships was leased to the Royal Navy in the summer of 1940. More would follow after Roosevelt's Lend-Lease Act was passed in the United States the following May. In the end, a total of 50 'Lend-Lease' destroyers were transferred. Their timely arrival helped stave off Britain's defeat in the war against the U-boats. They also bought time for her shipyards to finish building more escorts. The destroyers

HMS *Lewes* (G-68), namesake of the First Group of Towns, pictured here in 1941. Like her two sister ships, she was deployed as a North Sea escort. As the primary threat to her was from German E-boats or aircraft, she was rearmed accordingly. In late 1942 though, due to her poor mechanical state, she was reconfigured as an Air Target Ship.

were then followed by other smaller Lend-Lease warships, including over 100 frigates. Together, they not only helped Britain survive, but they also played no small part in turning the tide of battle in the Atlantic. Without them, Britain would almost certainly have lost the Battle of the Atlantic, and with it the war. These 50 rusty, obsolete little warships really did help save the world.

# DESIGN AND DEVELOPMENT

## The American destroyer fleet

The United States Navy rose to international prominence in 1898, following its victories at Santiago and Manila Bay during the Spanish–American War. In the process the country became a de facto imperial power, gaining new possessions in both the Caribbean and the Pacific. In the decade that followed the fleet was expanded, but while the US government cheerfully approved the building of new prestigious battleships, fewer resources were allocated to the construction of the smaller ships of the fleet. The result was an imbalanced fleet, when compared to those of the European naval powers of the period. The world cruise of the Great White Fleet in 1906–07 exemplified this emphasis on the battleship, as 16 of them took part in the circumnavigation, while the fleet's small force of 16 destroyers stayed at home.

It took a war scare with Japan in 1906–07 before the US Congress recognized the need for a more balanced navy. At that time the fleet's 16 destroyers were small vessels of less than 500 tons, designed to support the battle fleet in home waters. In 1908 though, the first of a more modern breed of destroyers was ordered. By the eve of World War I the US Navy boasted a force of 50 destroyers. The latest of these, the eight ships of the Cassin class, displaced over a thousand tons. Their role had changed too. These were now proper ocean-going destroyers, capable of protecting the battle fleet wherever it went. A contemporary school of thought, though, preferred smaller destroyers – more like torpedo boats – as these had a lower profile, making them better-suited to carrying out attacks on an enemy battlefleet. However, the US Navy favoured a different approach.

For them, the offensive capability of their new destroyers was secondary. Instead, the main role of US destroyers built before World War I was to protect the battlefleet from torpedo attacks by enemy destroyers or torpedo boats. That meant size, speed and guns were more important than their torpedo armament. For the Naval Board, the battlefleet was an integrated

The destroyer USS *Caldwell* (DD-69), namesake of her class, pictured in 1918 while serving as part of the US Navy's anti-submarine force based in Queenstown (now Cobh) in Ireland. At the time she was newly commissioned, and a useful addition to the US Navy's Atlantic Fleet. Four years later she would be 'mothballed' – placed in reserve – and in 1936 she was sold for scrap. Three of her sister ships though, were transferred to the Royal Navy.

The American-designed 4in guns mounted on the forecastle of a pair of Town-class destroyers. The narrow beam of these ships made serving the gun a challenge, particularly in heavy seas. Still, they were useful general-purpose weapons, and in most of these destroyers the forward 4in mounting was retained throughout the ships' wartime service.

formation, where each element in it would play its part. At its core though were the battleships, or dreadnoughts from 1906 onwards. The fleet's new breed of 'thousand tonner' destroyers were exactly that – they were there to protect the battlefleet, not carry out torpedo attacks on their own.

Still, the torpedo armament of US destroyers increased during this period, and by 1911, when the eight-ship Cassin class was ordered, they carried a respectable armament of eight torpedoes. At the same time they mounted 4in guns, compared to the 3in pieces employed in earlier destroyers. It was all part of the trend among the maritime powers of this period, where generally destroyers were becoming more powerful. The outbreak of a world war however changed the US Navy's attitude towards naval warfare. The old US Navy was essentially a peacetime organization. By 1916 though, it had been put on what was essentially a war footing, a move which reflected the growing realization that the United States might be dragged into the European war. This meant the fleet had to be restructured, modernized and expanded. Destroyers too, would have to become more adaptable.

## The 'flush-deckers'

By 1916 it was clear that German U-boats posed a major threat to British shipping. If the United States entered the war, this would become an American problem too. As a result, it was decided that American destroyers needed their own anti-submarine capability. Even in 1916 the US Navy had no means of detecting submarines, or of attacking them if they were submerged. No depth charges were carried. So, while these problems were addressed, the Navy Board busied itself re-evaluating the type of destroyers it needed. The last of the 'thousand tonners' were ordered in mid-1914, before the outbreak of World War I. The next batch, the six-ship Caldwell class, were authorized

 **TOWN-CLASS DESTROYERS HMS *SALISBURY* (1941) AND HMS *CLARE* (1941)**

**1.** The Town-class destroyer HMS *Salisbury*, formerly the Wickes-class destroyer USS *Claxton*, was part of the Second (*Campbeltown*) Group of 'four-stack' Lend-Lease Destroyers, transferred in early December 1940. She was modified for British use in Belfast. This view of her shows her as she looked in March 1941, after these were completed. This involved the removal of her 3in guns, and the replacement of her after 4in gun with a 12-pdr AA gun. Machine guns were mounted on her midships deckhouse on either side of her second funnel, next to her midships 4in guns. She still retained two triple torpedo tube mounts, and a pair of depth charge throwers were fitted aft. She carries a Type 286 surface-search radar at her masthead.

**2.** HMS *Stanley* was one of three Town-class destroyers to be converted into a Long Range Escort. The former Clemson-class destroyer USS *McCalla* was one of the Fifth (Bradford) Group of Town class vessels, but she and her sister ship *Bradford*, together with the Fifth Group destroyer *Clare* were considered robust enough to undergo the extensive refit required. She lost her two forward boilers and two forward funnels, which reduced her speed to 25kts, but created the space to store another 80 tons of fuel oil. Her forward superstructure was also modified to create a larger open bridge, with a Type 271 search radar mounted behind it, in its distinctive 'Chinese lantern' housing. Type 124 Asdic was also fitted. *Stanley* retained a triple torpedo tube mount, but her gun armament was reduced to a single 4in forward, and a 12-pdr AA mounting aft, backed up by two single 20mm Oerlikons. However, *Stanley*'s depth charge capacity was increased, and she carried eight depth charge throwers. Unlike *Bradford* and *Clare*, *Stanley* didn't have Hedgehog mounted in front of her bridge.

1

2

A pair of Lend-Lease destroyers pictured in Halifax, Nova Scotia, shortly after being transferred to the Royal Navy on 9 September 1940. They still bear their US pennant numbers, identifying them as the former USS *Aaron Ward* (DD-132) and USS *Abel P. Upshur* (DD-193). That day they were renamed the HMS *Castleton* and HMS *Clare* respectively.

the following spring, and while they followed the basic form of their predecessors, they were somewhat experimental, and so incorporated a number of important changes.

The first was designed to make these destroyers more seaworthy than their predecessors. While the 'thousand tonners' had a break in their hull aft of their forward superstructure, the Caldwells and those that followed them were flush-decked from bow to stern. This was an attempt to reduce rolling and pitching in heavy seas, but led to waves breaking repeatedly over the forecastle, rendering the forward gun all but unusable. The Caldwells also had a slightly wider beam than their predecessors, in an attempt to make them more stable. This, however, was traded off against a marginally shallower draught, and as a result they rolled more in a swell. It was soon found that the Caldwells, and their Wickes and Clemson-class successors, were 'wet ships', leaving their decks awash in even moderately rough seas.

The US Navy had already embraced the use of steam turbines in their destroyers, but the machinery used varied from class to class. With the six Caldwells, two different systems were used. The two built in the William Cramp yard in Philadelphia were fitted with three propeller shafts, powered by both high-pressure and low-pressure turbines, linked by gears, allowing high-speed performance as well as a more economical cruising one. In the other four ships though, a more conventional mechanical system was adopted, with two shafts, each linked to their own turbines. The two Cramp ships USS *Conner* and USS *Stockton*, as well as the USS *Gwynn*, were fitted with three 'stacks' (funnels), while the other three vessels had four of them. Both *Conner* and *Stockton*, as well as the USS *Craven*, would be transferred to the Royal Navy in September 1940, under the 'Destroyers for Bases' deal.

The first of these Caldwell-class 'flush-deckers' entered service in October 1917, five months after the United States' entry into World War I. The rest would follow them into commission before the end of the war. The building of the Caldwells had been authorized by Congress in the standard peacetime way, and due to their experimental nature work on them only began in the summer of 1916. By then, though, the National Defence Act of 1916 had been passed, and the US Navy began a dramatic expansion. The aim, according to President Woodrow Wilson, was to create 'the greatest navy in the world'. A parallel act funded a similar expansion by the US Army. While what was known as 'The Big Navy Act' approved the creation of a powerful battlefleet, it also included provision for the building of new destroyers.

What followed was the development of the US Navy's Wickes class of 111 destroyers. Together with the six preceding destroyers of the Caldwell class and the subsequent and even more numerous Clemson class of 136 destroyers, these would collectively form the Navy's fleet of modern 'four-stack' or 'flush-deck' destroyers. The numbers of ships involved were impressive – the bill's original quota was surpassed and then exceeded several times over. The reason was a realization that in order to operate in force in both the Atlantic and the Pacific, the US Navy needed far more destroyers than the bill had envisioned. This need was then doubled by the new requirement that destroyers provide anti-submarine protection for the battlefleet, and for America's merchant marine.

This dramatic production was made possible because the destroyers of the Wickes and Clemson class were designed for mass production. Seven shipyards were selected, two on the Pacific coast and the rest on America's Eastern Seaboard. The first of the Wickes class was laid down in June 1917, and the first launch took place that October. They were commissioned into service from the spring of 1918 onwards. The Wickes class destroyers were very similar to their 'four-stack' Caldwell-class predecessors. The main difference was that they were provided with an improved propulsion system, capable of producing a top speed of 35 knots. They also carried a geared cruising turbine on their port shaft for use at more economical speeds. Essentially then, they were an improved version of the Caldwell class.

Like their predecessors, the Wickes class destroyers were 'flush-decked'. A slight increase of beam and draught went some way to improving seakeeping qualities, but these were still wet ships, where all the gun positions and even the open bridge was frequently immersed by waves. Their improved propulsion system meant a greater displacement, but otherwise they were little different from the Caldwells. Another limitation was their range – 2,500nm at 20 knots. This though, varied widely from ship to ship, with the best being the ones built by the Bath Ironworks in Maine. Those were classed as 'Long Radius Boats'. Generally though, in terms of fighting power, these destroyers were little different from the 'thousand tonners' that came before. Still, in April 1917, when the United States entered the war, they were a welcome addition to the fleet.

In fact, none of the Wickes class were laid down before America went to war. So, it was up to the older 'thousand tonners' to support the Allies in the Atlantic, forming an anti-submarine flotilla which was based at Queenstown (now Cobh) in Ireland's County Cork from May 1917 onwards. It was only near the end of the war that the first of the 'four-stack' destroyers crossed the Atlantic to join the flotilla. When the war began, the US Navy still didn't have any anti-submarine weapons. Its Bureau of Ordnance began developing its own Mark I depth charges, but for the most part the fleet used modified British ones. By mid-1917 prototype depth charge racks were fitted to the destroyers of the anti-submarine flotilla, and these were followed by 'Y-guns', designed to project depth charges out onto the ship's beam. These anti-submarine weapons were then incorporated into the design of the 'four-stackers'.

The first two Caldwells would enter service in late 1917, but the last of them was only commissioned a few weeks before war's end. Production of the Wickes class was equally tardy. Only five of them were launched before the end of 1917, and despite the US Navy giving priority to destroyer production,

Upon reaching Britain, HMS *Castleton* (I-23), a Second (*Campbeltown*) Group destroyer of the Town class, underwent a very rudimentary Stage 1 modification in Devonport, and was sent off to sea again, joining the Western Approaches command. These modifications included removing her mainmast, her two after torpedo launchers and her bridge searchlights – all designed to reduce top hamper.

The Town-class destroyer HMS *Leeds* (G-27), formerly the Caldwell-class ship USS *Conner*, was one of three of the First (*Lewes*) Group, all of which were attached to the Rosyth Escort Force, for operations in support of North Sea Convoys. She though, suffered from chonic machinery failure, and spent more time under repair than at sea.

The repainting of the forward superstructure of a Town class of the Second (*Campbeltown*) Group. The ship's crest is probably that of HMS *Bath*, while the Norwegian crewmen indicate the photograph was taken in April 1941, when she was HNorMS *Bath*. Note the enclosed American-style bridge, surmounted by a signal platform and rangefinder.

of the 111 built only 25 were commissioned before the end of the war. By then a new class of 'four-stack' or 'flush-deck' destroyers had been commissioned. The 156-ship Clemson class was essentially an improved version of the previous class. The intention was to increase the range of these destroyers, and to improve their anti-submarine capability. A move to provide them with 5in guns was abandoned when the war ended, after just five of the destroyers were given them. Another experiment, giving the destroyers twin gun mounts, was also abandoned after just two ships were equipped with them.

The Clemson class destroyers had a similar speed to their predecessors – around 35 knots – and a similar range, despite attempts to increase this to almost 5,000 miles by adding additional fuel tanks. Like the other 'flush-deck' destroyers, the Clemsons were wet ships, and they rolled heavily in rough seas. Another problem they shared with their predecessors was that their tapered stern dug into the water, which increased the turning circle of the ship. This hindered their ability to manoeuvre tightly while carrying out depth-charge attacks. To compensate for this, the size of their twin rudders was increased slightly. However, all of these 'four-stack' cruisers had their faults, and they were generally seen as inferior to the British V&W-class destroyers being produced during the last years of the war.

**The mothballed fleet**

The sheer number of these destroyers was incredible – a total of 273 of them entering service with the US Navy between 1918 and 1922. By then however, the need for them had passed, and the new emphasis was naval disarmament and force reduction. This resulted in the Washington Naval Treaty of 1922. While primarily concerned with the reduction in size of existing battlefleets and limiting new construction, the treaty set the tone for a general scaling back of the US fleet. The older, smaller destroyers were disposed of shortly after the war, but the 'thousand tonners' and 'flush-deck' destroyers were retained. Many though, were laid up in reserve as soon as they were commissioned, and kept in 'mothballs' in anchorages on both the Atlantic and Pacific coasts, the largest of which were San Diego and Philadelphia.

In fact, as no new destroyers were designed and built for the US Navy until the early 1930s, they had to fill the gap during the interwar years. By 1930 though it was clear that the ageing condition of the remaining operational 'flush-deck' destroyers made it imperative that replacements be built. The eight destroyers of the Farragut class were authorized in early 1931, and would enter service during 1934–35. They marked the start of a rolling programme of destroyer building, with several more classes following in quick succession. These new warships would subsequently form the core of the US Navy's destroyer fleet during World War II. As a result, by the mid 1930s the 'thousand tonners' had been decommissioned and sold for scrap.

In San Diego, California, the berthing area for these decommissioned destroyers was known as 'Red Lead Row', due to the preserving paint used on the destroyers' decks. This picture was taken in 1922, but in the decade that followed many of them were either returned to service or sold for scrap.

Most of the remaining 'flush-deckers' were either mothballed, or, if deemed mechanically unreliable, they were disposed of. A few flitted in and out of commission during the 1930s, as new temporary roles were found for them. A few were still retained in service throughout the decade, deployed in secondary roles such as training or as vessels used by the US Naval Reserve. As a result, by the time war began in Europe the US Navy possessed a growing fleet of modern destroyers, as well as a sizeable number of obsolete 'flush-deck' ones, either fulfilling second-line duties or kept in mothballs. It was these that became the focus of British interest as the Battle of the Atlantic grew in intensity, and the shortage of anti-submarine escorts became critical.

## Destroyers for bases

In September 1939 the Royal Navy had a sizeable fleet of 184 destroyers, although only half of these were modern warships, built in the past ten years. The rest were of a similar vintage as the American 'flush-deck' destroyers, although some of these had been modified into anti-submarine escorts. Another 32 destroyers were under construction, together with another 20 smaller escort destroyers. The majority of these destroyers though, were not well-suited to the job of escorting convoys. They had been built as fleet destroyers, whose role was either to screen the battlefleet from attack, or to launch torpedo attacks against an enemy. Most destroyers therefore were attached to the Home or Mediterranean Fleet, and so were not readily available for convoy protection duties.

When the war began, Britain's lack of suitable convoy escorts became glaringly apparent. The fleet contained a number of small escort

HMS *Campbeltown* with HMS *Castleton* outboard of her, pictured in Halifax, Nova Scotia shortly after their transfer in early September 1940. They still bear the American pennant numbers of the USS *Buchanan* and USS *Aaron Ward*, which would remain until they were repainted in Devonport later that month.

This was a publicity picture, taken in Halifax, Nova Scotia, shortly before the first destroyer transfer on 9 September 1940. While British and American sailors examine a 4in gun, the USS *Buchanan*, USS *Crowninshield* and USS *Abel P. Upshur* astern of them are still flying their American colours. They would shortly become HMS *Campbeltown*, HMS *Chelsea* and HMS *Clare*.

vessels, mainly sloops. Thanks to the Emergency War Programme numerous small escort vessels were ordered, including over 50 corvettes, but it would take time for these to be completed and commissioned. In the meantime, poorly protected convoys were coming under attack from German U-boats operating in the Western Approaches to the British Isles. On 15 May – five days after the German invasion of France began – Prime Minister Churchill first asked President Roosevelt for the loan of 40 or 50 obsolete destroyers. This plea was repeated on 11 June – the day after Italy entered the war.

As Churchill put it: 'Nothing is so important for us to have the 30 or 40 old destroyers you have already had reconditioned. We can fix them very rapidly with our Asdics, and they will bridge the gap of six months before our wartime construction comes into play.' Four days later Churchill repeated the request, describing it as 'a matter of life and death'. King George VI then added his own personal plea to Roosevelt, adding: 'I well understand your difficulties, and I am certain that you will do your best to procure them for us before it is too late.' Roosevelt was sympathetic, but he had to tread carefully, as many of his countrymen favoured an isolationist stance. However, he had a political ace up his sleeve.

A deal was hatched whereby Britain would transfer control of several military bases in the Caribbean islands of Antigua, Jamaica, St Lucia and Trinidad, as well as in Bermuda, British Guiana and the Canadian island of Newfoundland. These would be transferred on a rent-free 99-year lease. In return, the United States would transfer control of 50 obsolete destroyers. They had already been assessed to have a scrap value of around $5,000 apiece. It was a deal that was considerably more beneficial to America than it was to Britain. It was, though, one that would prove crucial to Britain's survival in the face of the onslaught by Hitler's U-boats. On 3 September Admiral Stark, the US Chief of Naval Operations, officially declared that these destroyers were not crucial to American national security. Three days later, the first of the destroyers arrived in Halifax, Nova Scotia. Now it was up to the Royal Navy to transform these rusty 'four-stack' destroyers into working Atlantic escorts.

### In British service

The first of these destroyers to be handed over was the USS *Aaron Ward*, which reached Halifax, Nova Scotia, on 6 September. She was duly commissioned into the Royal Navy three days later as HMS *Aaron Ward*. All of these Lend-Lease destroyers would later be redesignated as Town-class destroyers, named after places in Britain or the Dominions whose names were also prevalent in the United States. She was sailed across the

HMS *Caldwell* (I-20), formerly the USS *Hale*, was a Second (*Campbeltown*) Group destroyer of the Town class, transferred in September 1940. She is pictured here in Plymouth Sound in late 1940, after undergoing her Stage 1 modifications in Devonport.

Atlantic by a British and Canadian crew, and reached Plymouth at the end of the month. After a minimal refit she was re-named HMS *Castleton* (I-23) on 2 October. The following month she sailed as part of the escort of Convoy OB-244. This pattern was followed by the other destroyers as they were handed over.

That September, 16 destroyers were handed over in Halifax, with another six earmarked for the Royal Canadian Navy. Another 18 followed in October, then five more in late November and a last batch of five in early December. In all, 44 Lend-Lease destroyers were transferred to the Royal Navy, and six to the Royal Canadian Navy, for a total of 50 warships. Of these, three were Caldwell class, 27 were Wickes class and 20 more were Clemson class. The six transferred to the Canadians were made up of four Wickes-class (*Haraden*, *Mackenzie*, *Thatcher* and *Williams*) and the two Clemson-class destroyers *Bancroft* and *McCook*. These six would become the *Columbia*, *Annapolis*, *Niagara*, *St Clair*, *St Francis* and *St Croix* respectively. That left the three Caldwells, 23 Wickes and 18 Clemsons for the Royal Navy. The British divided their 44 acquisitions into five groups:

| Group 1 Town class (Lewes group) | 3 Caldwell-class destroyers |
|---|---|
| Group 2 Town class (Campbeltown group): | 12 Wickes-class destroyers |
| Group 3 Town class (Bath group): | 11 Wickes-class destroyers |
| Group 4 Town class (Belmont group): | 7 Clemson-class destroyers |
| Group 5 Town class (Bradford group): | 11 Clemson-class destroyers |

The performance of the Wickes and Clemson classes varied slightly, depending on which years they were built in and how they were modified during their American careers. This grouping kept destroyers with similar characteristics together. The main parameters here were speed, fuel capacity and endurance. This grouping then, helped the Royal Navy assign these newly acquired destroyers to appropriate duties. The next task was to convert the old destroyers for British use, and to reflect the new convoy escort roles they would be given. Generally, most of these destroyers were modified as

HMS *Castleton* (I-23), on the day of her commissioning into the Royal Navy in Halifax, on 9 September 1940. Her rust-streaked appearance bears testimony to her recent service on neutrality patrols in the Gulf of Mexico and Florida Strait, operating from Key West in Florida.

described in the next chapter. However, some are worth noting separately, as they were treated differently from their consorts.

Three of the Clemson-class (or Town class – *Belmont* and *Bradford* groups) destroyers, HMS *Bradford*, HMS *Clare* and HMS *Stanley* (formerly the USS *McLanahan*, USS *Abel P. Upshur* and USS *McCalla*) were more extensively modified into long-range escorts. The two foremost boilers and their funnels were removed, to make room for extra fuel tanks and improved accommodation. Their bridges were extended, and *Clare* had her beam 4in guns replaced by single 2-pdrs. As the war progressed, further modifications were made to these Lend-Lease destroyers. In most cases this involved the upgrade of radar suites, with Type 290 or Type 291 fire control radar replacing the Type 286 at the masthead, and HF/DF antennae fitted to the top of the mainmast. In many cases, from 1943 onwards, Hedgehog mortars were added in the forecastle. In all cases these later modifications were made during scheduled periods of refit or repair. All these Towns were never particularly good anti-submarine escorts. Their poor turning circle made them unwieldy, and their armament was ill-suited to escort work. Still, they made up for this by their very presence at a crucial stage of the U-boat war. While most of their turn of speed wasn't important in convoy work, it came into its own when hunting U-boats – allowing them to reach the scene of a submerged U-boat quickly, to then be detected and attacked. The Admiralty's Department of Naval Construction though, had reservations about all of these American-built destroyers. They saw them as inherently unstable due to excessive topweight. So, many of these British modifications were done to improve stability as well as to tailor the ships' armament to suit their new-found purpose as dedicated anti-submarine escorts.

**B**  **HMS *STANLEY* ATTACKING A U-BOAT, DECEMBER 1941**

HMS *Stanley*, formerly the USS *McCalla*, was one of three US Clemson class destroyers to be converted into Long Range Escorts. On 14 December 1941 she left Gibraltar as part of the homeward-bound convoy HG-76, made up of 32 merchantmen. *Stanley*, commanded by Lt Cdr David Shaw, was part of an especially strong escort, commanded by Cdr 'Johnnie' Walker. On the morning of 17 December a patrolling fighter from the escort carrier HMS *Audacity* spotted a U-boat on the surface, some 22 miles to port of the convoy. Walker sent part of the escort to attack her. Kapitanleutnant Baumann's *U-131* dived when the warships approached, and went deep. An initial depth charge attack by the warships the escort destroyers HMS *Blankney* and HMS *Exmoor* and Walker's sloop HMS *Stork* was unsuccessful. So, Walker ordered *Stanley* and the Flower class corvette HMS *Penstemon* to attack too. This shows *Stanley* dropping a pattern of ten depth charges over the contact, guided by *Penstemon*, lying off to maintain a good Asdic contact. Afterwards contact was lost, and Walker rejoined the convoy, leaving *Stanley* and *Penstemon* to continue the search for the elusive U-boat. In fact *U-131* had been badly damaged in the attack, and a little later she was forced to surface, when she was sunk by gunfire from the British escorts. Baumann and all but one of his crew though, lived to tell the tale, and were taken prisoner. Two nights later though, in the early hours of 19 December, *Stanley* was torpedoed by Oberleutnant Gengelbach's *U-574*, and blew up and sank, taking all but 25 of her crew with her. Walker then forced *U-574* to the surface before ramming and sinking her.

## The Captain class

As the war progressed and the Battle of the Atlantic continued unabated, the US Navy began transferring other warships to the Royal Navy and the Royal Canadian Navy. These included escort carriers, minesweepers, coastguard cutters and even a few submarines. The most numerous though were frigates. With a disregard for the niceties of grammar, the US Navy called these destroyer escorts. These were markedly different from the Royal Navy's own Hunt-class escort destroyers, as they were slower and were specifically designed as anti-submarine escorts. So, the Royal Navy re-classified them as frigates. When transferred to Royal Naval service in 1943–44, these small warships were given a minimal modification – usually just the addition of a 2-pdr gun at the bow, as a defence against German E-boats.

There were 78 of them in all, 32 turbo-electric destroyer escorts of the US Navy's Evarts class, and 46 diesel-electric powered ones of the Buckley class. Together they formed the Royal Navy's Captain class of frigates, divided into two groups, according to their propulsion systems. The Evarts class of destroyer escort was developed after the US Navy realized it needed large numbers of anti-submarine vessels and convoy escorts. This had been discussed before America's entry into the war in December 1941, but no concrete proposals had been developed. It was increasingly clear though, from watching the British struggle to protect their convoys, that these vessels would be vital if the US Navy were to take a more belligerent role in the Battle of the Atlantic.

In early 1941 plans were developed for a small destroyer, around 280ft long, and armed with a pair of 5in guns, torpedo tubes and depth charges. These though, were never developed, as the US Navy preferred to build full-size destroyers, which could perform a greater range of roles. That summer though, the British requested an extension of the Lend-Lease scheme, to provide up to 100 of these new escort vessels. On 15 August Roosevelt agreed to provide 50 of them, even though, at the time, these ships only existed on paper. The Royal Navy was then invited to assist in the design process. The first real problem to overcome was finding a suitable propulsion system. The US Navy was already being expanded, and there was a shortage of suitable steam turbines. So, the US Navy's Bureau of Ships turned to diesel engines, of the kind used in US submarines.

These ships were then referred to as BDEs (British Destroyer Escorts), which reflected the significant British influence in producing the specifications of these vessels. One of the main requirements was that these miniature destroyers could be built quickly, and in large numbers. The actual plans though, were drawn up by the American naval architects Gibbs & Cox. In the end, the BDEs would be fitted with a pair of Winton diesel engines produced in Cleveland, Ohio, by a diesel engine division of General Motors. Like submarines, these were supported by an electric drive system produced by General Motors. The original

The short-hull frigate HMS *Bayntun* (K-310) was the first of the Royal Navy's new Captain class to enter service. After being commissioned in Boston in January 1943, she, 'worked up' in Bermuda, and then crossed the Atlantic to join the Western Approaches Command. Before the war's end she would be credited with the sinking of four U-boats.

The USS *Evarts*, the first of the US Navy's fleet of hundreds of wartime destroyer escorts, was the namesake of the class the Royal Navy dubbed Captain class (short hull or diesel-electric). Essentially, *Evarts* was designed as a collaborative Anglo-American effort, drawing on hard-won British experience gained during the first years of the Battle of the Atlantic. The result was an escort vessel that was ideally suited to its wartime role.

plan was to provide two diesel engines per shaft, but other wartime demands meant that in the end only single engines were fitted. This resulted in BDEs only being able to make around 20 knots. That though, was all the British really needed for a mass-produced convoy escort.

Following America's entry into the war the US Navy also adopted the BDE design, and in early 1942 a large number of orders was placed for these destroyer escorts. By then these were also classified as the GMT class, referring to General Motors Tandem – a reference to their diesel-electric propulsion system. The lead ship and namesake of the Evarts (GMT) class was launched on 7 December 1942 – the anniversary of Pearl Harbor – and the USS *Evarts* entered service with the US Navy in April 1943. In the end, 97 of these Evarts-class escorts would be built, of which 32 were transferred to the Royal Navy. The rest served in the US Navy. This though, fell short of the original British plea for 100 escorts. So these Evarts were followed by the next large group of American-built destroyer escorts, the Buckley (TE) class.

The Buckleys were slightly larger than the Evarts, but had a smaller displacement. This was partly due to their propulsion system, a pair of General Electric steam turbines and two boilers, driving two shafts, supported by an electric drive system. The result was a more impressive maximum speed of 23 knots. This, however, came at the cost of a slightly reduced range. These were classed as the TE class, for Turbine Electric. The first of these escorts was laid down in mid-1942, and the namesake of the class, the USS *Buckley*, was launched in January 1943. A total of 154 of them entered service with the US Navy, and another 46 of the Buckleys were transferred to the Royal Navy.

Changing their designation from destroyer escort to frigate was largely due to their armament. Despite their original specifications, the first of these American-built destroyer escorts didn't carry torpedoes, and were given a relatively puny main armament of 3in guns. The Admiralty already had a ship type called the 'escort destroyer', and these American newcomers were notably different from these more powerful British Hunt-class escorts. As a result, they were reclassified as frigates, which better suited their characteristics.

As well as changing their designation, the British also modified these new acquisitions, when they were handed over. This though, compared with the Town-class destroyers, was a much less extensive procedure, and a far more organized one. These ships began to enter service with the Royal Navy from January 1943. They arrived at a critical time in the war against the U-boats, and were usually used to form hunting groups, designed to take the fight to the enemy. By war's end they had accounted for 30 U-boats.

The building of destroyer escorts in the Bethlehem Hingham Shipyard, near Boston Massachusetts. The hull plates on the right probably mark the beginning of HMS *Calder* (K-349) which was launched in March 1943 and commissioned less than four months later. Next to her is a Buckley class sister ship earmarked for the US Navy. She would be commissioned as the USS *Foss*.

# ROYAL NAVAL EMPLOYMENT

### Modifications

When these Town-class destroyers were handed over, they had to be converted to suit the needs of the Royal Navy. First though, they were all surveyed by Admiralty inspectors, who noted their often extensive list of structural or mechanical problems. These would be dealt with in the ship's first refit.

HMS *Georgetown* (I-40) was a Town class destroyer of the Third (*Bath*) Group, operated as part of the Western Approaches Command, serving in the North-West approaches. In late 1942 she was transferred to the Royal Canadian Navy for a year, before being placed in reserve. She is pictured here in mid-1943, while in Canadian service.

Otherwise they would be built into the ship's rolling maintenance programme. As for the modifications, these were divided into two stages. The most pressing modifications dealt with stability. The British considered the 'four-stackers' as having too much topweight, which reduced their stability. This then, together with improving the ships' anti-submarine capability, would form the core of the initial Phase 1 refit, undertaken when the ship reached Britain.

Further modifications were designated Phase 2. These would improve the fighting potential of these destroyers, but weren't considered vital. So, they would be left until the ship needed to go into port for a scheduled refit, or for repair. This however, didn't always happen, and some of the Towns never underwent more than their initial Phase 1 refit. Even this wasn't carried out as consistently as the Admiralty inspectors would have liked. A lot depended on the availability of weapons or parts, and the time available for the job. At the time, all British shipyards were working at full capacity, so anything resulting in unnecessary delay was postponed until a later refit. As a result it is almost impossible to list exactly what modifications were done to each ship. In general though, the modifications were as follows:

### Initial refit (Phase 1) modifications
- Fitting of British Asdic (sonar), complete with underwater dome.
- Fitting of British Mark IV depth charge throwers and extended depth charge racks.
- Removal of the two after (triple) torpedo launchers.
- Removal of after 3in and 4in/50 guns. The 4in gun in 'X' mount was removed altogether, and replaced by a British 12-pdr 12cwt QF high gun. The 3in/23 gun on 'Y' mount was also removed.
- Removal of waist 4in/50 guns. These were meant to have been replaced by quadruple 0.5in machine guns, but this wasn't always carried out. If available, they were replaced by single 20mm Oerlikon light AA guns in each mounting, rather than by machine guns.
- Removal of the mainmast, and shortening of the foremast.
- Shortening of the three aftermost funnels.

All of these Phase 1 modifications were supposed to be undertaken on all of the Town-class destroyers which entered British service. In practice though, due to urgent operational needs, some of the first destroyers to be delivered were rushed into service with only minimal conversion. So, uniformity was never achieved. In some of the later Phase 1 refits a Type 271 surface search radar was added if available. In general though, as long as stability and anti-submarine capability were improved, the destroyers were deemed fit for service, and sent to join the escort fleet.

In the Leeds group – the old US Caldwell-class destroyers, made up of HMS *Lewes*, HMS *Leeds* and HMS *Ludlow* (formerly the USS *Conway*,

USS *Conner* and USS *Stockton*) both 'A' and 'Y' guns were removed, leaving just the two beam-mounted 4in guns. All torpedo tubes were also taken away. In HMS *Lewes* though, all of her 4-in guns were removed, and were replaced by 2-pdr or 20mm light AA guns. Incidentally, both *Leeds* and *Ludlow* had a three-shaft propulsion system, and only had three funnels. HMS *St Albans* also lost all of her torpedo tubes.

The Group One (*Lewes*) Town-class destroyer HMS *Lewes* (G-68), pictured while serving with the Rosyth Escort Force. Her 4in guns were removed, and instead, in a raised platform below the bridge, she carries two 2-pdr 'pom-poms', which were better suited to action against enemy E-boats. Note her enlarged open bridge, atop her American-style enclosed one.

Phase 2 modifications were carried out during subsequent refits. At this point any Phase 1 modifications which hadn't been done were completed. Then the following changes were made:

- Removal of the remaining two triple torpedo tube launchers, and replacing them with a single triple torpedo launcher mounted on the centreline.
- Fitting a Type 271 surface search radar if not already carried, and a Type 286 air search radar. The first was mounted above the bridge, and the second in the foremast.
- Any remaining beam-mounted 4in/50 guns were removed, and replaced by single 20mm Oerlikons.
- Propeller guards were replaced with stronger ones.

In addition, if possible, the American heavy ships' boats and davits were removed, and replaced by lighter British equivalents. Also, where possible the searchlight platform was lowered, and in some cases moved further aft. In many cases the bridge structure was modified to accommodate a British-style open bridge rather than an American closed one.

By the time the first of the Captain-class frigates entered service, a far more organized system of modifications had been drawn up. After all, the British had been involved in the design of these ships, and knew roughly when they would be handed over. These modifications were undertaken in Belfast. For the most part this involved the increase of depth charge capacity, British Asdic sets, a director control tower added abaft the bridge and extra light anti-aircraft guns. To make them better suited to the Atlantic, their bilge keels were also lengthened to improve their seakeeping qualities. When the first Buckleys appeared they carried a launcher with three torpedo tubes, mounted amidships. These were therefore removed to reduce tophamper, as there was no need for them in convoy escorts. Generally though, modifications to the American-built destroyer escorts was a simple and relatively speedy process.

HMS *Crowninshield*, still sporting her American colour scheme and pennant numbers, pictured as she entered Plymouth Sound on 28 September 1940 – 19 days after her handover. On arrival she was renamed HMS *Chelsea* (I-35), and after a Stage 1 modification she was sent out to join the Western Approaches Command.

## Deployment

Like their six Canadian sister ships, the majority of the 44 Town-class destroyers acquired by the Royal Navy were destined

In March 1941 HMS *Newport*, a Third (*Bath*) Group ship was transferred to the Royal Norwegian Navy, becoming HNorMS *Newport*. Unusually, her pennant number has not been painted on her hull. She is pictured lying in the River Foyle, near Londonderry, which served as her base while serving with the Western Approaches Command.

to become convoy escorts. A number though, were earmarked for minelaying duties. Essentially, they were allocated to one of three operational commands:

1. The Rosyth Escort Force

These escorted North Sea convoys, passing up and down Britain's eastern seaboard. All three Group 1 (*Lewes*) destroyers were transferred to this command. Others were temporarily attached from Western Approaches Command when available.

2. Western Approaches Command

Based in Liverpool, this Command dealt with all Atlantic convoy operations, as well as the Gibraltar convoys. It also provided escorts, when required, to the Sierra Leone convoys or 'WS' convoys, linking Britain to West Africa, South Africa, Egypt and the Suez Canal, and India. The majority of the Royal Navy's Lend-Lease Town-class destroyers served with the Western Forces Command, and so were heavily involved in transatlantic convoy escort duties.

In the North Atlantic the escort forces assigned to convoy escort duties were divided into:

- The Mid-Ocean Escort Force – operating between St Johns in Newfoundland and Londonderry in Northern Ireland.
- The North-West Approaches – operating between the mid-Atlantic and the convoy's British port. For the most part these destroyers were based in Londonderry or Liverpool.
- The Newfoundland Escort Force – operating between St Johns and a designated point in mid-Atlantic.
- The Western Local Escort Force (WLEF) – providing escorts for shipping operating between New York and St Johns. This was a Canadian designation, and involved both British and Canadian escorts. In early 1942 this was combined into one command with the Newfoundland Escort Force.

### TOWN CLASS DESTROYERS HMS *RAMSEY* (1942) AND HMS *GEORGETOWN* (1942)

**1.** HMS *Ramsey*, formerly the Clemson class destroyer USS *Meade*, was transferred in November 1940, becoming one of 13 ships of the Fifth (*Bradford*) Group. She was modified in Portsmouth, and then in February 1941 she was attached to the Liverpool-based 5th Escort Group. However, in late 1941 she returned to Boston to undergo a more extensive Stage 2 refit. This shows her as she looked afterwards, while serving as an Atlantic escort. She was plagued by mechanical trouble though, and underwent frequent repairs. In August 1943, *Ramsey* was withdrawn from front-line service, and became an Air Target Ship. Here though, in her prime, she carried three 4in guns and a 12-pdr. Mounted aft, a pair of single machine guns amidships, and a single triple torpedo tube mounting. She also carried a Type 271 surface search radar abaft her bridge, and a Type 286 air warning radar atop her foremast.

**2.** HMS *Georgetown*, formerly the Wickes class destroyer USS *Maddox*, was transferred in September 1940, and was designated a Group 3 (*Bath*) vessel. In November she underwent a limited Stage 1 modification in Devonport, then went off to join the 4th Escort Group. *Georgetown* remained on duty with the Western Approaches Command until late 1941, when she underwent a more extensive Stage 2 modification. This shows her when she resumed convoy work the following April. She now carried only one 4in gun forward, and a 12-pdr AA gun aft. She also retained a triple torpedo launch mounting aft and four 20mm Oerlikons. Her depth charge racks and two depth charge throwers aft were augmented by a Hedgehog ASW projector forward of her bridge. She also had a Type 271 surface search radar abaft her bridge and a Type 291 air search radar in her foremast, as well as an HF/DF radio-direction finder and an improved Type 141A Asdic set.

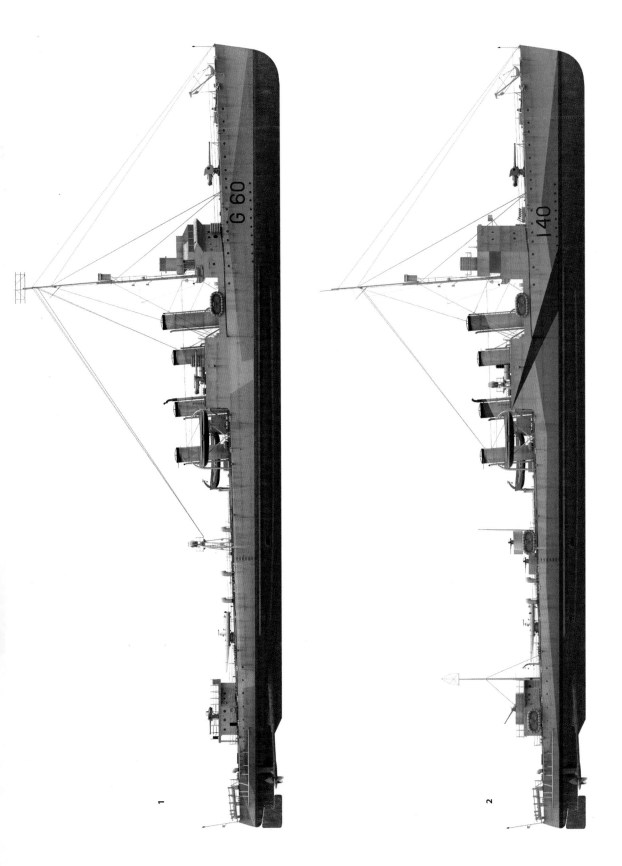

1

2

Of these, the majority of Town-class destroyers were assigned to the first of these forces, and so escorted their charges all the way across the Atlantic, or else covered south-bound convoys bound for Sierra Leone, venturing as far as either the Azores or Freetown. Some also provided protection to the Gibraltar convoys, operating between Gibraltar and Liverpool.

### 3. The 1st Minelaying Squadron

Based at the Kyle of Lochalsh on the west coast of Scotland, this squadron maintained the Northern Barrage, a series of minefields deployed between Orkney, Shetland, the Faroes and Iceland. The Group 3 (Bath)

HMS *Campbeltown* undergoing extensive modification before the St Nazaire raid of March 1942. The idea was to make her resemble a German Mowe-class torpedo boat, by removing her two after funnels, raking the two others, and replacing her armament with a single 12-pdr and eight 20mm Oerlikons, seen here on bandstand mountings.

destroyers *Bath*, *Brighton*, *Charlestown*, *Lancaster*, *Newark*, *St Albans* and *St Marys* provided anti-submarine protection for the minelayers, when not called away on more conventional escort duties. Also deployed with the minelaying squadron were the Group 2 (Campbeltown) destroyers *Castleton* and *Wells*. When the squadron was disbanded in July 1943, these destroyers were either sent to join the Rosyth Escort Force, or were placed in reserve.

For the most part the six Canadian destroyers remained in Canadian waters, protecting the approaches to Newfoundland. Several of the Royal Navy's Town-class destroyers were later transferred to the Royal Canadian Navy, as well as other Allied navies:

| To the Royal Canadian Navy (RCN) | |
| --- | --- |
| *Buxton* | August 1942 |
| *Caldwell* | July 1942 |
| *Chelsea* | November 1942–July 1944 |
| *Hamilton* | June 1941 |
| *Leamington* | November 1942–July 1944 |
| *Lincoln* | July 1942–August 1944 |
| *Mansfield* | September 1942 |
| *Montgomery* | December 1941 |
| *Richmond* | June 1943–June 1944 |
| *Salisbury* | September 1942 |
| *Georgetown* | September 1942 |

| To the Royal Netherlands Navy (RNeN) | |
| --- | --- |
| *Campbeltown* | March 1941 |

| To the Royal Norwegian Navy (RNoN) | |
| --- | --- |
| *Bath* | April 1941 |
| *Lincoln* | February 1942–August 1944 |
| *Mansfield* | December 1940–September 1942 |
| *Newport* | March 1941–June 1942 |
| *St Albans* | April 1941–July 1944 |

| To the Soviet Navy (returned in 1949) | | | |
|---|---|---|---|
| Ship | From | Transferred | Soviet Name |
| Churchill | RN | July 1944 | Deyatelny |
| Chelsea | RCN | July 1944 | Derzky |
| Roxburgh | RN | August 1944 | Doblestny |
| St Albans | RNoN | July 1944 | Dostoyny |
| Lincoln | RCN | August 1944 | Druzny |
| Brighton | RN | July 1944 | Zharky |
| Leamington | RCN | July 1944 | Zhguchy |
| Richmond | RCN | June 1944 | Zhivuchy |
| Georgetown | RCN | August 1944 | Zhyostky |

The first Town-class destroyer to be deployed operationally was HMS *Caldwell*, in late October 1940. For the most part, from late 1940 on, these destroyers were formed into Escort Groups which were assigned as a unit to particular convoys as their escort force. *Caldwell*, for example, became part of the 5th Escort Group. Others formed part of the 1st, 2nd, 4th, 5th, 6th and 7th Escort Groups during 1941 and 1942. These deployments tended to continue until individual ships were temporarily detached from their group to undergo refit or repair, or to undergo additional training at Tobermory, where the Western Approaches' anti-submarine school was located. Refits were either undertaken in British shipyards, usually commercial ones, or in those on the Eastern Seaboard of the United States.

Some ships moved from one command to another. For example, in late 1940 HMS *Lancaster* was attached to the 1st Minelaying Squadron, but from 1941 on she was occasionally attached to the Western Approaches Command, escorting transatlantic convoys as they neared the British Isles. Then, in the late summer of 1943 she became part of the Rosyth Escort Force, and operated in support of North Sea Convoys until the end of the war. Essentially, the Towns were assigned wherever they were needed the most. For example, HMS *Salisbury* was taken off regular Atlantic convoy duty to escort War Special (WS) Convoys, bound for the Middle East by way of the Cape of Good Hope. She protected them as far as Freetown in West Africa. Later she even ventured into the Western Mediterranean, protecting Malta relief operations. Similarly, in July 1942 HMS *Leamington* was one of the few Towns to take sail in the Arctic Convoy, forming part of the escort for the ill-fated Convoy PQ-17.

By 1943 though, many of these Towns were showing their age, and the effect of near-constant exposure to Atlantic weather. By the end of the year, only 16 of these Lend-Lease destroyers were still in active service as convoy escorts. The remainder were either placed in reserve due to their poor mechanical condition, or relegated to secondary roles. Since entering service many had experienced a host of mechanical problems, and had to spend lengthy spells under repair. Typical problems included engine or boiler defects and extensive leaks through bursting hulls. Many of those that were still fit for service were therefore eventually given less mechanically demanding roles. Many became Air Target Ships, used to train Fleet Air Arm and Royal Air Force air crews in anti-shipping operations. Generally though, their time as active warships was all but past.

The short-hull Captain-class frigate HMS *Drury* (K-316) was commissioned in Philadelphia in April 1943, and spent the entire war with the same commander, Lt Parker. It subsequently saw service in both the Atlantic and the Mediterranean. During the war it was involved in the sinking of two U-boats, in November 1943 and April 1945.

## KEY

1 Depth charge rack (one of two) –

2 After deckhouse

3 Single 12-pdr. AA gun mounting

4 After (emergency) steering position

5 Engine room hatch (one of two)

6 Searchlight platform

7 Ship's motor whaleboat and davits (one of two)

8 Funnel (one of four – after one shortened)

9 Single 4 in./50 gun mounting (one of two – port and starboard wing)

10 Galley (atop midships gun platform)

11 Type 286 air search radar antenna

12 Foremast (ladder access to foretop lookout position)

13 Signal platform – single 0.5in. machine gun on each wing

14 Radio direction finding loop, with rangefinder forward of it

15 Enclosed bridge

16 Single 4 in./50 gun (forward)

17 Capstan and anchor cables

18 Anchor (one of two)

19 Forward fuel tanks

20 Forward magazine

21 Midships fuel tanks

22 Boiler room containing two boilers (one of two - forward and after)

23 Engine room containing a geared turbine engine (one of two – forward and after)

24 After fuel tanks

25 After magazine

26 Store room

27 Propeller, shaft and rudder (set of two)

28 Propeller guards (one of two – on each quarter)

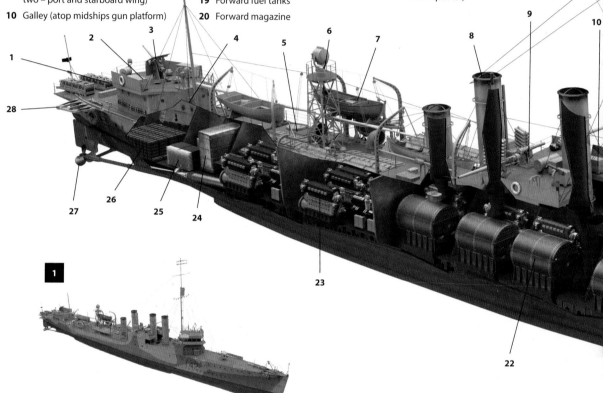

## HMS *CAMPBELTOWN* (TOWN-CLASS DESTROYER, 1941–42)

The old 'four-stacker' USS *Buchanan* was one of the first of the 50 Lend-Lease destroyers to be handed over to the Royal Navy, becoming HMS *Campbeltown*. In October 1940 she was modified in Gosport, then sent off to Liverpool to join the 17th Flotilla, of the Western Approaches Command. Her career got off to a bad start, as thanks to her dreadful steering system she was in two collisions, the last of which resulted in three months of repair. Then, in March 1940 she was handed over to the Royal Norwegian Navy. From April onwards, she and her Norwegian crew formed part of the 7th Escort Group, operating in support of Atlantic convoys. She was re-crewed by the Royal Navy in September, and subsequently operated on the convoy route between Britain and Sierra Leone. At the end of the year though, she returned to Gosport for repairs. It was there that she was earmarked for Operation *Chariot* – the raid on St Nazaire. The old destroyer was modified again, stripping her down to her basics. Then, on 26 March she left Falmouth, her hull laden with high explosives. Her job was to ram the dock gates in St Nazaire, rendering the dock useless. She rammed them at 01.38 on 28 March, but her charges didn't detonate – at least not right away. They finally detonated at noon, tearing her apart, killing hundreds of onlookers, and putting the dock out of action for the rest of the war. As a result, the battleship *Tirpitz* was denied a vital Atlantic base.

This illustration shows *Campbeltown* as she looked in late 1941, during her time protecting the Sierra Leone convoys. Her camouflage scheme during this period can be seen more clearly in the smaller, lower left view of *Campbeltown* (1). The smaller views of the destroyer in the lower right show her as she looked as: (2) the USS *Buchanan*, shortly before being handed over to the Royal Navy and (3) *Campbeltown* as she appeared during the St Nazaire raid of March 1942.

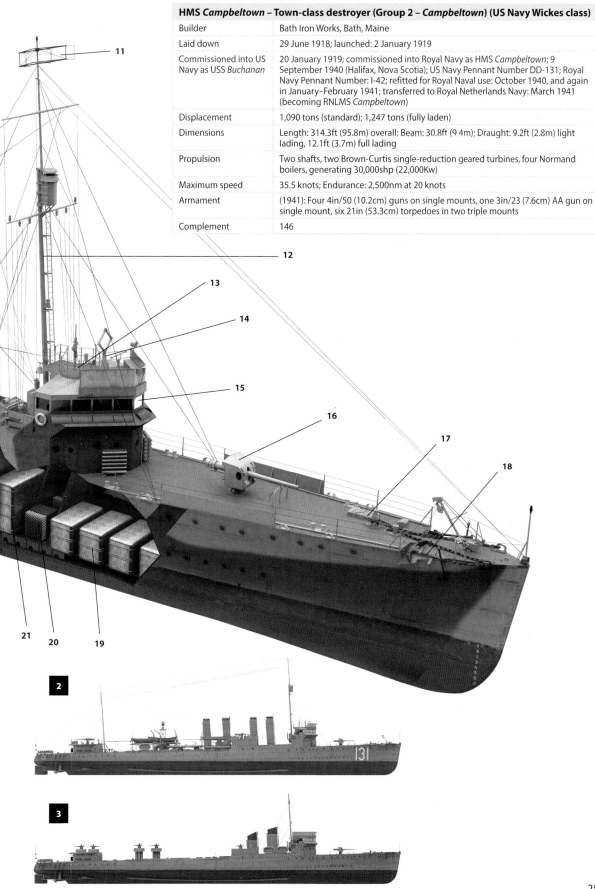

| HMS *Campbeltown* – Town-class destroyer (Group 2 – *Campbeltown*) (US Navy Wickes class) | |
|---|---|
| Builder | Bath Iron Works, Bath, Maine |
| Laid down | 29 June 1918; launched: 2 January 1919 |
| Commissioned into US Navy as USS *Buchanan* | 20 January 1919; commissioned into Royal Navy as HMS *Campbeltown*; 9 September 1940 (Halifax, Nova Scotia); US Navy Pennant Number DD-131; Royal Navy Pennant Number: I-42; refitted for Royal Naval use: October 1940, and again in January–February 1941; transferred to Royal Netherlands Navy: March 1941 (becoming RNLMS *Campbeltown*) |
| Displacement | 1,090 tons (standard); 1,247 tons (fully laden) |
| Dimensions | Length: 314.3ft (95.8m) overall; Beam: 30.8ft (9.4m); Draught: 9.2ft (2.8m) light lading, 12.1ft (3.7m) full lading |
| Propulsion | Two shafts, two Brown-Curtis single-reduction geared turbines, four Normand boilers, generating 30,000shp (22,000Kw) |
| Maximum speed | 35.5 knots; Endurance: 2,500nm at 20 knots |
| Armament | (1941): Four 4in/50 (10.2cm) guns on single mounts, one 3in/23 (7.6cm) AA gun on single mount, six 21in (53.3cm) torpedoes in two triple mounts |
| Complement | 146 |

The Captain-class frigate HMS *Bazely* (K-311) was of the short-hull (or Evarts class) group, powered by diesel-electric engines. After entering service in February 1943 she served with an escort group, and during her wartime career was involved in the sinking of three U-boats, two in late 1943 and one in 1945.

Fortunately, by then a new type of Lend-Lease convoy escort had entered service – the Captain-class frigate. These began entering service in number during early 1943, and by that autumn a steady stream of them were joining the fleet. This placed a great demand on the Royal Navy's pool of available manpower, which in part explained the impetus to withdraw the worst of the Towns from service. Instead, their now experienced crews could be used to leaven the mass of inexperienced 'Hostilities Only' seamen sent to man the Captains.

On reaching Britain, these American-built destroyer escorts were reclassed as frigates, and modified in Belfast for British use. They were then attached to the Western Approaches Command. Most were allocated to Escort Groups (EGs). The 4th EG was the first to be made up exclusively of Captain-class frigates. As they entered service other Captains would form the 1st, 3rd and 5th Escort Groups, and later the 15th and 21st Escort Groups. Yet more were allocated to other Escort Groups which were made up of other warships, rather than just Captains.

Others still were attached directly to naval commands responsible for local convoy protection, such as the Nore Command, or to the Channel Flotillas of the Portsmouth and Devonport Commands, during the preparations for the Normandy invasion.

| Captain-class frigate attachments, 1943–44 | |
|---|---|
| 1st EG | *Affleck, Balfour, Bentley, Capel, Garlies, Gould, Gore, Hoste* (briefly) and *Whitaker*. |
| 3rd EG | *Berry, Blackwood, Cooke, Domett, Duckworth, Essington, Braithwaite* and *Rowey*. |
| 4th EG | *Bazeley, Bentick, Byard, Calder, Drury* and *Pasley*. Also (briefly) *Blackwood* and *Burges*. |
| 5th EG | *Aylmer, Bickerton, Bligh, Grindall, Keats, Kempthorne, Tyler* and *Goodson*. |
| 10th EG | Included *Bayntun, Braithwaite* and *Foley*. |
| 15th EG | *Dacres* (briefly), *Inglis, Lawson, Loring, Louis, Moorston, Mounsey* and *Narborough*. |
| 17th EG | Included *Burges, Cranstoun, Stockham* and *Moorsom*. |
| 18th EG | Included *Hoste* and *Balfour*. |
| 19th EG | Included *Bullen, Cotton* and *Goodall*. |
| 21st EG | *Byron, Conn, Deane, Fitzroy, Redmill* and *Rupert*. |
| Nore Command | *Cubitt, Curzon, Cosby, Dakins, Ekins, Holmes, Rutherford* and *Halsted*. |
| Portsmouth and Gosport Command | *Hotham, Narborough, Rupert, Waldengrave, Spragge* and *Rowley* (mid-1944). |

The Nore Command, while primarily responsible for protection of the shipping in the North Sea and English Channel, was also expected to support the Normandy invasion when the time came. The Command's frigates then, were grouped into the 16th (Sheerness) and 21st (Harwich) Destroyer Flotillas before the summer of 1944. Their task was to prevent U-boats from harassing the Normandy landings from the east, while the Portsmouth and Devonport frigates would do the same on the western side of the Channel. In addition, *Dacres, Kingsmill* and *Lawford* were earmarked as Headquarters ships during the invasion, operating off the invasion beaches.

The need to protect the invasion armada was a major consideration for Operation *Neptune* – the amphibious component to Operation *Overlord*, the Normandy invasion. The threat of interference by German U-boats led to the deployment of the Captains from the Nore, Portsmouth and Gosport Commands on either flank of the landing area. The threat posed by E-boats and other small torpedo craft was countered by deploying Allied coastal forces craft in large numbers. These would need support though, and would have to be coordinated. As a result, another group of Captains were designated as Coastal Forces Control Frigates (CFCFs), to strengthen and control these flotillas of smaller Coastal Forces craft. *Duff, Riou, Retalick, Seymour, Stayner, Thornborough, Torrington and Trollope* were all designated as CFCFs for Operation Neptune. After the invasion they would be joined by *Cubitt, Rutherford, Dakins* and *Ekins*. It is fair to say that without the presence of all these frigates, Operation *Neptune* could never have been carried out without significant Allied losses.

## CAPABILITY

Above all else, these Lend-Lease destroyers and frigates were anti-submarine warships, whose role was to protect convoys, and to hunt and sink enemy U-boats. In some cases though, as in the destroyers of the Rosyth or Nore commands, they might also come up against enemy coastal force vessels, such as E-boats. While they maintained a modicum of surface weaponry, to engage surfaced U-boats or to fend off E-boats, their key offensive components lay on their quarterdeck, or in an Asdic dome beneath their hull. All the anti-submarine weaponry in the world was of little use if the enemy couldn't be detected. Asdic (or sonar) therefore was of vital importance. It seems that when they were handed over, some of the 'flush-deck' destroyers carried World War II era hydrophones – a passive underwater listening system. It seems unlikely they carried any form of echo-ranging equipment – the US Navy's precursor to sonar. So, fitting Asdic sets was of crucial importance.

This shows the Town-class destroyers HMS *Georgetown* (left) and HMS *Roxburgh* in dry dock, probably during their repairs in a Clydeside shipyard in July 1941. The propeller and rudder arrangements on these Town-class destroyers meant they had a very large turning circle – a hindrance when hunting U-boats.

Essentially, Asdic was a means of detecting submerged submarines using pulses of sound. A high-frequency pulse would be sent out, and would then be reflected by the submarine. The reflected pulse would be picked up by a quartz transducer. By measuring the time taken to 'ping' the pulse out and back, the distance to the submarine could be calculated. The system was first developed during the last year of World War I, and by 1940 it had evolved into a reliable but not infallible device, which when linked to a recorder could measure range, bearing and speed of the submerged target. It had drawbacks though – it could only work at speeds below 18 knots, and it demanded skill by the operator to tell the difference between a U-boat and a shoal of passing fish.

For the most part the Town-class destroyers of all groups were fitted with Type 141 Asdic sets during their initial refit. This may have been an adaptation of existing American echo-ranging sets by adding British range and bearing recorders.

These had a theoretical detection range of around 700yds, in ideal conditions, and with a skilled Asdic operator at hand. It was only when these destroyers underwent their Phase 2 modification refit that a streamlined Asdic dome was fitted underneath the vessel's hull. This was the most effective means of sending out and receiving a sound beam, but the time involved in adding it to the newly acquired ships prevented it being included in the Phase 1 modifications. These modifications converted the set into a Type 144A, which had an improved range of around 1,000yds. By contrast, the later Lend-Lease Captain-class frigates were fitted with a Type 123 or Type 127 Asdic set, which had a theoretical detection range of up to 1,500yds.

HMS *Clare* (I-14) was another of the three Town-class destroyers turned into Long Range Escorts. They were given an improved anti-submarine capability, and extra fuel tanks. In October 1942, after this photograph was taken, a Hedgehog ASW projector was mounted in *Clare*, immediately in front of her bridge, and aft of her forward 4in gun.

The standard British Mark VII depth charge resembled an oil drum, packed with 200lb of high explosive. These were either rolled off a rack fitted at the stern of the escort, or else launched off the beam of the ship using a depth charge thrower. Usually a combination of stern-dropped and beam thrown charges was used, to create a 'pattern'. The charges were rigged to detonate at a pre-set depth of between 50ft and 400ft, and each had a lethal blast radius of around 20–25yds. The frigates though, also carried a Mark XI Hedgehog, an ahead-throwing weapon which launched a pattern of small projectiles into the water ahead of the escort, which detonated when they struck a U-boat.

In all anti-submarine attacks the weak point came when the escort was almost on top of the target. Then, due to the angle of the Asdic beam, contact

**E** **TOWN-CLASS DESTROYERS HMS *LEWES* (1943) AND HMS *RIPLEY* (1943)**

**1.** HMS *Lewes* was one of the three destroyers of the Town-class First (*Lewes*) Group. This made her one of the oldest of the 50 Lend-Lease destroyers to be transferred into British ownership. Formerly the Caldwell-class USS *Conway*, she was commissioned into the Royal Navy in October 1940. She and her three sisters were all modified on arrival in Britain, and were employed as part of the Rosyth Escort Force, charged with escorting North Sea convoys up and down Britain's east coast. However, service was delayed until early 1942, due to damage sustained in an air raid on Devonport. This shows her as she looked in early 1942, once she finally reached Rosyth. By then her original armament had been removed. She now carried three 3in guns amidships and aft, a pair of 2-pdr. 'pom-poms' abreast of each other forward of the bridge, and two 20mm Oerlikons on bandstand mounts amidships. For ASW work she only carried a single depth charge rail, and a pair of depth charge throwers. Her only radar was a Type 291 air warning set, mounted in her foremast. That December she was withdrawn from service, and sent to South Africa, to serve as an Air Target Ship. This meant bomber crews could practise anti-shipping strikes on her.

**2.** HMS *Ripley* was a Town-class Fifth (*Bradford*) Group destroyer, and was formerly the Clemson-class vessel USS *Shubrick*. She underwent her Stage 1 modification in Devonport, and in early 1941 she joined the 5th Escort Group, attached to the Western Approaches Command. *Ripley* underwent her Stage 2 modification in late 1942. This shows her after she resumed her escort duties in May 1943. She now carried a heavily modified and reshaped bridge, and was armed with a 4in gun forward, a 12-pdr. aft, and three 20mm OErlikons amidships. Her ASW weapons consisted of a Hedgehog ASW projector forward, beneath the bridge, two depth charge racks aft and four depth charge throwers. She carried a Type 271 surface search radar abaft the bridge, a Type 291 air warning radar atop her foremast, and an HF/DF radio-direction finder on a specially rigged mast aft. A smaller MF/DF set was attached to the front of her bridge.

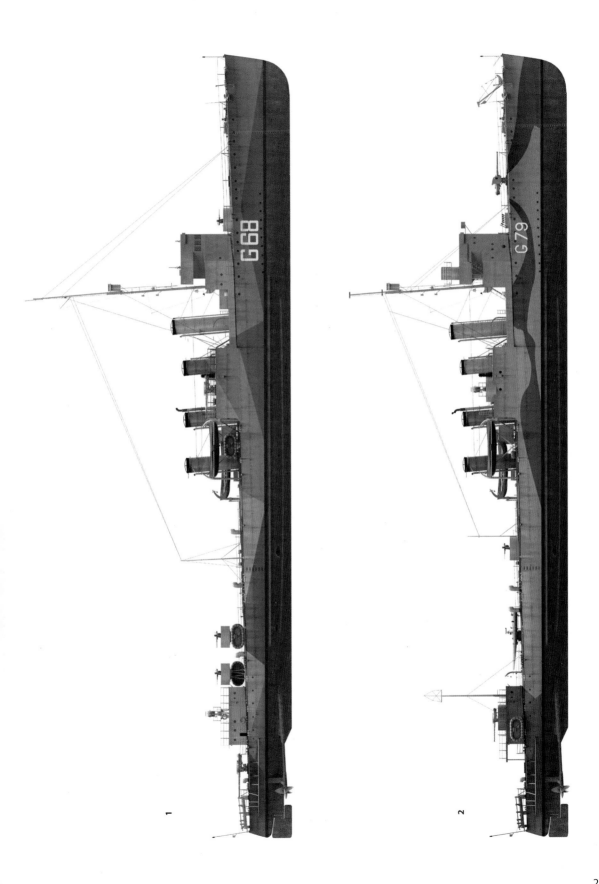

1

2

HMS *Holmes* (K-581) was a long-hull Captain-class frigate, the equivalent of the American Buckley class of destroyer escorts. Many of the crews of the Captain class preferred the American name for their ship type, as it sounded more dashing. *Holmes* spent much of the war performing convoy escort duties, but also saw service off Normandy, protecting the supply lines to the Allied beachhead.

with the boat was lost. This gave the U-boat commander a chance to get out of the way of the depth charges. The solution was to hunt in groups. If one or two escorts detected a submerged U-boat, then they would use their radios to guide their companions onto the target. This way, in theory, there was no way the U-boat could evade its pursuers. In practice though, the boat could hide between different layers of salinity, or lie on the bottom and hope the pursuers would lose contact and give up the hunt.

The other useful tool in the frigates was the Hedgehog, a multiple spigot mortar which could fire its projectiles up to 200yds (183m) ahead of the ship. These were housed in a box-style launcher mounted in front of the frigate's bridge. When fired, its 24 projectiles landed in a 40 yard (37m) diameter circle. Each projectile carried a 35lb (15.9kg) high-explosive charge, which detonated on contact, unlike depth charges which exploded at a set depth. Each frigate carried several reloads for the Hedgehog, making it a versatile and effective weapon.

For the most part though, U-boats hunted on the surface. Their speed on the surface was around 14 knots – more than double their submerged speed. In the dark they might be able to creep close to a convoy without being detected. For the escorts, the real game-changer here was radar, or radio-direction finding as the British still called it in 1940. Most of the Towns were eventually fitted with Type 271 radar, a surface-search set that was capable of detecting surfaced U-boats at a range of up to six miles. The Captain-class frigates carried the American SC set, which had similar, but slightly improved, range. To augment detection at night, two 24in searchlights were fitted, mounted abaft the bridge and on a platform near the after deckhouse.

Once detected on the surface, the escort would use its surface guns to engage the U-boat. The American-built 4in/50 Mark 12 gun had a range of 16,200yds (14,800m) at 20 degree elevation, and could fire high-explosive (HE) rounds, while the 3in Mark 14 gun was a small anti-aircraft gun, with a range of 10,100yds (9,240m) at 65 degrees of elevation. It could also fire starshells. A US Bausch and Lomb rangefinder was mounted on the signal platform above the bridge, to direct the fire of the 4in guns. The Mark 8 torpedoes had a range of 16,000yds (14,600m) at a speed of 36 knots, and carried a warhead containing 466lb of high explosive. Finally, light anti-aircraft machine guns and 20mm Oerlikons provided basic close-range defence against aircraft, but their effectiveness was limited.

The Captains mounted US-made 3in/50 Mark 21 guns, which were capable of engaging both air and surface targets. They had a range of 16,600yds (13,350m) at an elevation of 43 degrees, and could theoretically fire up to 15 rounds a minute. They were provided with a range of semi-armour piercing (SA), HE and anti-aircraft rounds, as well as illumination rounds. They were linked to a British fire direction tower, which included rangefinding equipment, which made these guns reasonably effective, despite their small calibre. Although a decent anti-aircraft weapon, it was really too small to engage surface targets with any chance of causing significant damage, other than by a lucky hit on a submarine's conning tower.

# LIFE ON BOARD

The Lend-Lease Town-class destroyers were almost universally disliked by their crew. Their ageing hulls were plagued by leaks, particularly through corroded rivets. Elsewhere, leaks were found in the hulls and even through internal bulkheads. This, combined with their notoriously wet decks when in any kind of a sea made these vessels damp both inside and out. Their crews almost universally hated their 'four-stackers'. Their narrow beam and heavy tophamper meant they rolled viciously, making them extremely uncomfortable. In a strong Atlantic gale they were positively dangerous. Several had their bridges and upperworks damaged by heavy seas, or fittings attached to rusty decks washed over the side. Some even had officers and men crushed and killed during Atlantic storms.

The ice-covered Town class destroyer HMS *Leamington* (G-19), a Second (Campbeltown) Group vessel, pictured arriving in Halifax, Nova Scotia in December 1942. She was subsequently transferred to the Royal Canadian Navy, becoming HMCS *Leamington* of the Newfoundland (later Halifax) Escort Force.

Their obsolete steering gear regularly broke down, and when functioning this was so inefficient that it gave the destroyers a similar turning circle to a battleship. Numerous Town-class destroyers were in collisions during their service, whether with other escorts or with the merchantmen they were there to protect. Steering failures in bad weather risked the ship broaching, and even capsizing in rough seas. Lt Cdr Hill, who commanded one during 1942–43 said afterwards, 'It seemed to me that all of my previous experience was just a preparation for my time in HMS *Mansfield*.' He went on to describe the sacrificing of HMS *Campbeltown* by blowing her up against the lock gates of the dry dock in St Nazaire as 'the best thing that could have happened to the Town-class destroyers'.

Their crews spoke of a myriad of electrical and wiring defects, faulty machinery that was at the end of its useful life and an awkward messing layout, with the accommodation divided by the engine room. Movement between the forward and after parts of the ship had to be done via the upper deck, which in heavy seas was often dangerous. This was made even worse by the vicious rolling these destroyers were prone to. Admiral Tovey, commander of the British Home Fleet at the time, said of them, 'I thought they were the worst destroyers I have ever seen – poor seaboats, with appalling armament and accommodation.' They were described as incredibly uncomfortable to live aboard, and everything from washing facilities and 'heads' (toilets), the condition of the crewmen's messdecks and storage space was deemed sub-standard.

Some of the crew of a short-hull Captain-class frigate, skylarking for the camera during operations off the Normandy coast in the summer of 1944. The assortment of 'rig' is typical of wartime escort crews, where uniformity was considered less important than practicality and comfort. This photograph also gives a good view of the arrangement of the 20mm Oerlikons mounted amidships, around the funnel.

A group photograph of the crew of the Captain-class (short hull) frigate HMS *Bazely*. At their centre is the ship's first commanding officer, Acting Lt Cdr Jeffry Brock RCNVR, a Canadian officer who had already commanded two smaller escorts. *Bazely* had a crew of around 200 officers and men.

It was often impossible to keep clothing or personal possessions dry, and crewmen spoke of sea water sloshing around on the deck, beneath their hammocks, either from leaks or being brought down the hatches from the sea-washed upper decks. One American officer described the leaky hulls as 'just thick enough to keep out the water and small fish'. It seemed as if sometimes they couldn't even do that. Even the galley was located on the upper deck amidships, between the third and fourth funnels. Even if the cooking facilities worked properly, moving food and drink from them to the messdecks or wardroom was often a dangerous business. One historian, James Lamb, described them as 'the most dubious gift since the Trojan Horse'. Many of their crews would probably agree.

By contrast, the Captain-class frigates were extremely popular with their crews. It took time to get used to unfamiliar American equipment, particularly the turbo-electric or diesel-electric propulsion systems, but once mastered these proved relatively straightforward to operate. Far more impressive though, was the accommodation on board these frigates. Living space was far in advance of contemporary Royal Navy standards. Every sailor had his own bunk, arrayed in three tiers, rather than a hammock. This avoided the business of lashing up and stowing bedding every morning. In previous British warships meals were centrally cooked in the galley and then taken to the individual messdecks to eat – a practice which had existed since the age of sail. In the Captains though, American-style cafeteria-style messing was used. Meals were prepared in the galley, and then served through a hatch into a messhall. The galley had modern equipment: fridges, dishwashers and even an ice-cream maker.

There were other unheard of luxuries too. In most British warships, laundry was done in buckets on the washrooms or messdecks. In the Captains though, the ships had small laundries, where clothes could be washed

### HMS *TROLLOPE* IN ACTION WITH E-BOATS, JUNE 1944

The Captain-class frigate HMS *Trollope* was commissioned in Boston on 10 January 1944 when Lt Cdr Harry Westacott assumed command of her. She then crossed the Atlantic, and was modified in Gosport before joining the fleet. In late April she became a Coastal Forces Control Frigate (CFCF), supporting anti E-boat patrols off Cherbourg. *Trollope* was involved in one small skirmish, but her real test came in early June, during Operation *Neptune* – the amphibious part of the D-Day landings. On the night of 6–7 June she formed the outer picket of a patrol line protecting the shipping lying off the beachheads. That night the 5th S-boot (E-boat) Flotilla based in Cherbourg attempted to attack, but came up against a cordon of Allied warships. *Trollope* was the outlying 'picket' boat that evening, and detected the approaching E-boats on her radar. She fired off starshells, then engaged the six boats with her guns. Three E-boats turned away but the others headed straight for her. *Trollope* fired with everything she had, including her bridge-mounted Lewis gun. Two E-boats were hit, with one stopped and set ablaze and another badly damaged. If they launched torpedoes at *Trollope*, these went by unseen in the dark. The third boat then broke off the attack. None of these E-boats though, made it past the Allied cordon that night, to reach the anchored ships beyond. *Trollope* survived her first baptism of fire, but a month later wasn't so lucky. On 6 July, during another night-time clash, the frigate was torpedoed by an E-boat, and although beached near Arromanches, she was deemed a 'constructive loss'.

much more efficiently. These ships also contained unbelievable luxuries to the wartime British sailor, such as chilled drinking water fountains and individual large steel storage lockers. In the Towns, as in all contemporary British destroyers or frigates, storage space was in small bench lockers, where space was at a premium. For the sailors, this was luxury indeed. Facilities for senior rates and officers were even more impressive, save for the toilet facilities, which were deemed primitive, and had to be upgraded during a Phase 2 refit. All in all though, the crew were delighted with the facilities in their new ships.

For the most part, both the Towns and the Captains were crewed by 'Hostilities Only' (HO) ratings. Many, when they joined their first escort ship, had never set foot in a warship before. These were augmented by a handful of old hands. As war losses mounted, the number of veteran pre-war sailors dwindled, as did the number of experienced reservists. So, in both the Towns and the Captains, a very thin leavening of experienced hands and senior rates had to teach these newcomers their trade. Basic training only went so far. Much depended on the men's willingness to learn 'on the job'. Fortunately, most were keen to learn, if for no other reason than their own survival might depend upon it. By 1942–43, most were every bit as good as regular pre-war seamen.

Also, by the time the Captains entered service, a sizeable number of HO ratings had gained the experience they needed to become senior rates. This gained experience was particularly true in the more specialist skills on board – marine or electrical engineering, electronics, including Asdic and radar operation and maintenance, and in weaponry. The ship's senior officers were for the most part experienced men, with the leadership qualities to turn their ship into an efficient fighting unit. While escort work was not seen as a good career move in the pre-war Navy, as promotion was better in larger ships, this attitude changed by 1942. The increasing professionalism of anti-submarine work and the challenges presented to escort commanders made these posts much more popular – and even a stepping stone to higher things.

Many junior officers though, were often sent to sea with only a modicum of training. A sizeable number of them joined from the Royal Naval Reserve or Royal Naval Volunteer Reserve, so while they had maritime experience of some kind, they were unused to the ways of the Navy. They too had to learn their trade while at sea. This included gaining bridge watchkeeping certificates, learning the basics of man management and leadership, and even Naval etiquette. Therefore, a lot of responsibility lay on the shoulders of both the senior officers and experienced senior rates to show these newcomers 'the ropes'. In almost every case it worked, and these ships' companies quickly settled down to become efficient and skilled escort crews. It helped of course, that for most HO ratings they remained with the same ship throughout the entire war.

A wartime convoy, viewed from the stern of a Town-class destroyer. A fighter from an escort carrier flies overhead, looking for surfaced U-boats. In the destroyer the layout of the depth charge racks is clearly visible, each capable of holding six charges. The wooden frame between them is a temporary installation, designed to provide the crew with a more stable footing when handling the charges.

# ESCORTS IN ACTION

The most famous Lend-Lease warship of the war was undoubtedly HMS *Campbeltown*, formerly the USS *Buchanan*. Her story though, and the part she played in the St Nazaire raid of 28 March 1942 has already been described in detail (*see* CAM 192 *St Nazaire 1942*). She is also the subject of a plate in this book, so a description of her explosive end is not really necessary here. After all, it was an atypical use for a Lend-Lease warship. Better instead to concentrate on what these warships were more normally used for – anti-submarine work. Looking then, at both a typical Town-class destroyer and a Captain-class frigate in action might be a more useful use of space here. For this, both HMS *Stanley* and HMS *Bentinck* fit the bill perfectly.

The bridge of HMS *Campbeltown*, pictured during preparations for the St Nazaire raid (Operation *Chariot*), carried out in Devonport. Campbeltown was probably selected as she had spent extensive time in repair since her transfer into British service.

HMS *Stanley*, formerly the USS *McCalla*, was handed over to the Royal Navy in October 1940. She was extensively modified in Devonport the following year, and in August she was sent to join the Western Approaches Command. She was subsequently sent as an escort to convoys operating on the Sierra Leone route, and first saw action that October. In December 1941 she arrived in Gibraltar, to join the escort of Convoy HG-76, which was bound for Liverpool. She sailed with the 32-ship convoy on 14 December, as part of a particularly strong escort force, led by Commander 'Johnnie' Walker. The convoy was targeted by Wolfpack *Seeräuber*, and the first attack took place two days into the voyage. The convoy battle that followed is described in detail by Osprey in *The Convoy*. This following description though, describes a typical anti-submarine operation conducted by a Town-class destroyer.

The convoy escort included the auxiliary carrier HMS *Audacity*. At 0900hrs on 7 December 1941 a Martlet fighter from the tiny carrier spotted a U-boat on the surface, 20 miles from the convoy. This was reported to Walker, who sent *Stanley* to attack it, accompanied by the escort destroyers *Blankney* and *Exmoor*, and the corvette *Penstemon*. Walker then followed in his sloop *Stork*. The U-boat dived when they approached, but at 1000hrs the two escort destroyers carried out depth charge attacks in the area. Then Lt Cdr David Shaw arrived in *Stanley*, followed by the corvette and the sloop, and the escorts began a more methodical search. An Asdic contact was made by *Penstemon* at 1036hrs, and Walker ordered the corvette to carry out a depth charge attack, followed by *Stanley*. Both dropped a pattern of ten depth charges, half at 150ft and the rest at 400ft. Afterwards though, no oil or wreckage was detected, so it was considered unlikely the U-boat had been hurt.

Contact was lost again, so Walker led *Stork* and the two escort destroyers back to rejoin the convoy, leaving *Stanley* and *Penstemon* to continue the search. In fact, the U-boat had been damaged in the joint attack. Kapitänleutnant Baumann's *U-131* was now lying still at her maximum safe depth of 200m, a little distance from the two escorts. Her hydrophones had been knocked out, and she was leaking. After 70 minutes Baumann decided he needed to surface to save his crew. When the U-boat broached the surface she was spotted by Shaw, who radioed Walker. He then turned

HMS *Stanley* (I-73) was one of three former Clemson-class destroyers which were converted into Long Range Escorts. In December 1941 *Stanley* formed part of the escort of Convoy HG-76, and was instrumental in the sinking of a U-boat. Two days later though, she was torpedoed and sunk by a member of the same *Seeräuber* wolfpack.

towards the U-boat, lying a mile away, and ordered *Stanley*'s bow 4in gun to open fire. The U-boat tried to get way on the surface, and even managed to shoot down a Martlet fighter that came too close. However, she had no real chance to escape.

*Stanley* was soon joined by the two escort destroyers, and the three warships pounded the surfaced U-boat, scoring several hits. Then the crew began abandoning ship. *Stanley* and her consorts kept firing though, until at 1321hrs the bows of the U-boat reared up out of the water, and she slipped under. All that remained was to pick up the oil-soaked survivors. Amazingly, only one of the U-boat's crew had been killed in the action. *Stanley* had to share her victory with the four other escorts. Other attacks took place during the days that followed, and early in the morning of 19 December *Stanley*'s luck ran out. She was torpedoed by a U-boat, and exploded in a fireball. She sank within minutes, taking all but 25 of her crew with her. Commander Walker though, exacted revenge just minutes later, when he rammed and sank the attacker, Oberleutnant Gengelbach's *U-574*.

Just over four years later, on 26 January 1945, the 4th Escort Group were busy undertaking a sweep of the Irish Sea to the east of Wexford, in Ireland's County Cork. Shortly after dawn a radio report came in that the Captain-class frigate HMS *Manners* had been attacked and damaged to the east of Dublin, some 75 miles to the north. Commander Garwood, commander of 4th EG, had three Captains under his immediate command – his own ship HMS *Bentinck*, as well as HMS *Aylmer* and HMS *Calder*. So, he decided to see what he could do to help.

**G** **CAPTAIN-CLASS FRIGATES HMS *GOODALL* (1944) AND HMS *BENTINCK* (1944)**

**1.** The short-hull Captain-class frigate HMS *Goodall* had originally been laid down as the Evarts-class destroyer escort USS *Reybold*, but was transferred to Royal Naval ownership after her launch in Boston Navy Yard. She was commissioned in October 1943, when Lt Cdr Fulton RNVR became her commanding officer. He would remain her commander until she was torpedoed and sunk by *U-286* off Murmansk during the closing days of the war. She began active service in March 1944, as part of the B6 Escort Group, which covered Atlantic convoys. She then transferred to the 19th Escort Group, which protected the Arctic Convoys. This shows her as she looked when she joined the B6 EG. As well as her standard 3in armament, *Goodall* carried a twin 40mm Bofors gun forward, and nine 20mm Oerlikons. Her ASW armament consisted of a Hedgehog ASW projector, two depth charge racks and eight depth charge throwers. She carried American SL surface search and SC air warning radars.

**2.** HMS *Bentinck* was a long-hull Captain-class frigate, of the US Buckley class. She entered British service in May 1943, and after being modified for British use she was attached to the 4th Escort Group that autumn, serving as the group lead ship. She was deployed on convoy escort duties, primarily in support of the Arctic Convoys. However, in late 1944 the 4th EG was deployed to home waters, based in the Irish Sea. In January *Bentinck* took part in the sinking of *U-1051* off the Isle of Man, and three months later she had a hand in the sinking of *U-774* and *U-636* to the west of Ireland. This shows the frigate as she appeared when she first joined 4th EG. She is armed with three 3in guns, three 40mm Bofors and eight 20mm Oerlikons, as well as the usual suite of two depth charge racks, eight depth charge throwers and a Hedgehog ASW projector. Like *Goodall*, she carried a pair of American SL and SC radars.

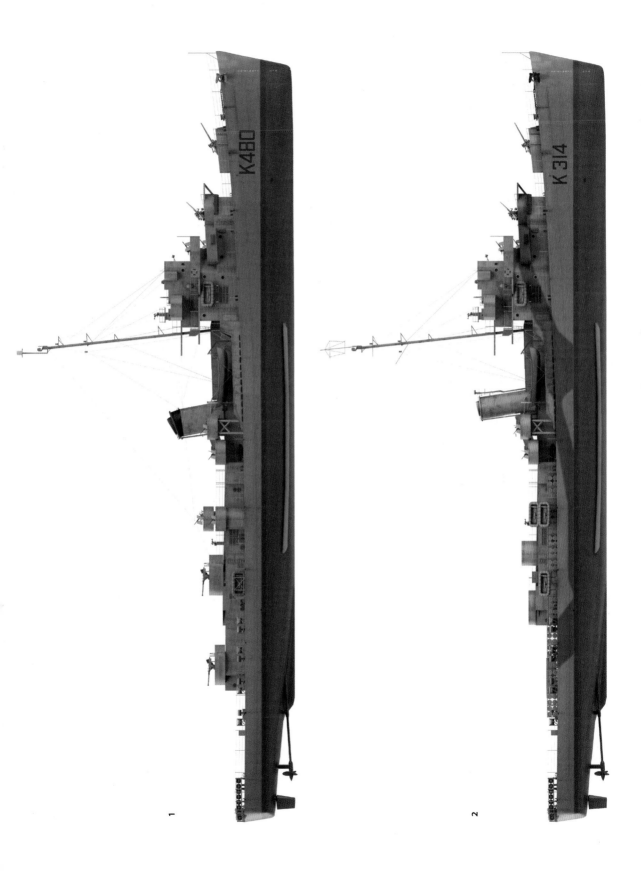

1

2

Effective U-boat hunting relied on maintaining good communications between the hunting warships. During an attack the radio operator would help the commander of the warship, 'pinning the U-boat' with Asdic to guide the other warships over the contact, to carry out their attack.

This picture of HMS *Campbeltown* was taken by a German photographer during the forenoon of 28 March 1942, with the old destroyer stuck fast against the dock gates of St Nazaire. A few minutes later the charges in her hull detonated, ripping *Campbeltown* apart, and wrecking the dry dock.

The 4th EG set off northwards at full speed to help, and three hours later they found *Manners* still afloat, but badly crippled, with her stern blown off. She was roughly halfway between Dublin and the southern tip of the Isle of Man, some 20 miles south of the island. When they arrived, Lt Cdr Waterhouse of *Manners* told Garwood that he had a firm Asdic contact that morning, and was planning to carry out an attack when his frigate was hit. He suspected the U-boat was still somewhere in the vicinity. As a result, when the 4th EG arrived on the scene, Garwood ordered them to carry out a thorough Asdic search. Sure enough, a contact was quickly made. Without doubt she was the U-boat that had torpedoed the *Manners*.

Being the closest to the contact, Garwood's *Bentinck* carried out an immediate depth charge attack, plastering the area with multiple depth charge patterns of five charges apiece. No hits seemed to have been made though, and contact was lost. Garwood therefore handed the search over to Lt Cdr Playne of *Calder*, and *Bentinck* took the crippled *Manners* under tow. She then set off towards Barrow-in-Furness, 85 miles away to the east. Neither Playne in *Calder* nor Lt Campbell in *Aylmer* managed to detect the U-boat. Then, Playne had an idea. Using his echo sounder he began a methodical echo sounder survey of the seabed. Sure enough, he detected what appeared to be a U-boat, sitting on the seabed. Playne then carried out a carefully calculated Hedgehog attack, using Asdic to guide him over the target.

The U-boat was damaged, and rose to the surface a mile off the frigate's starboard beam. Campbell in *Aylmer* was also nearby. He immediately turned his frigate towards the U-boat, and ordered her to make full speed. He then rammed the wallowing U-boat amidships. The U-boat sank immediately, taking her entire crew of 44 men with her. *Aylmer* had a wrecked bow, and her Asdic dome had been sheared off, but Campbell felt it was worth it. He then followed Bentinck and Manners to Barrow, accompanied by *Calder*.

It transpired that the U-boat was U-1051, commanded by Oberleutnant von Holleben. She was on her first war patrol when she was sunk with all hands. It was a confusing little engagement, with all four frigates sharing the credit for the sinking – one of the last of the war. It though, demonstrated how teamwork and methodical searching could achieve results. They, after all, were what anti-submarine warfare was all about.

# THE SHIPS

## Destroyers

### Town class (Group 1 – *Lewes*) – formerly US Caldwell class – 3 ships in group

| HMS (Pennant No.) | US Navy Name | Builder | Launched | Commissioned (US Navy) | Commissioned (Royal Navy) | Fate |
|---|---|---|---|---|---|---|
| *Leeds* (G-27) | *Conner* | Cramp | August 1917 | January 1918 | | Broken up 1947 |
| *Lewes* (G-68) | *Conway* | Norfolk | June 1918 | October 1918 | October 1940 | Scuttled 1946 |
| *Ludlow* (G-57) | *Stockton* | Cramp | July 1917 | November 1917 | | Sunk as target practice 1945 |

Cramp: William Cramp & Sons, Philadelphia, PA
Norfolk: Norfolk Navy Yard, Norfolk, VA

### Town class (Group 2 – *Campbeltown*) – formerly US Wickes class – 12 ships in group

| HMS (Pennant No.) | US Navy Name | Builder | Launched | Commissioned (US Navy) | Commissioned (Royal Navy) | Fate |
|---|---|---|---|---|---|---|
| *Campbeltown* (I-42) | *Buchanan* | | January 1919 | January 1919 | | Lost 28 March 1942 |
| *Caldwell* (I-20) | *Hale* | Bath | May 1919 | June 1919 | September 1940 | Broken up 1945 |
| *Castleton* (I-23) | *Aaron Ward* | | April 1919 | April 1919 | | Broken up 1947 |
| *Chelsea* (I-35) | *Crowninshield* | | July 1919 | August 1919 | | Broken up 1949 |
| *Lancaster* (G-05) | *Philip* | | July 1918 | August 1919 | | Broken up 1947 |
| *Leamington* (G-19) | *Twiggs* | New York | September 1918 | July 1919 | | Broken up 1951 |
| *Lincoln* (G-42) | *Yarnall* | Cramp | June 1918 | November 1918 | October 1940 | Broken up 1952 |
| *Mansfield* (G-76) | *Evans* | Bath | October 1918 | November 1918 | | Broken up 1944 |
| *Montgomery* (G-95) | *Wickes* | | June 1918 | July 1918 | | Broken up 1945 |
| *Richmond* (G-88) | *Fairfax* | Mare Island | December 1917 | April 1918 | | Broken up 1949 |
| *Salisbury* (I-52) | *Claxton* | | January 1919 | September 1919 | December 1940 | Broken up 1944 |
| *Wells* (I-95) | *Tillman* | Charleston | July 1919 | April 1921 | | Broken up 1945 |

Bath: Bath Iron Works, Bath, ME
New York: New York Shipbuilding Corporation, New York, NY
Mare Island: Mare Island Navy Yard, Vallejo, CA
Charleston: Charleston Navy Yard, Charleston, NC

### Town class (Group 3 – *Bath*) – formerly US Wickes class – 11 ships in group

| HMS (Pennant No.) | US Navy Name | Builder | Launched | Commissioned (US Navy) | Commissioned (Royal Navy) | Fate |
|---|---|---|---|---|---|---|
| *Bath* (I-17) | *Hopewell* | Newport | June 1918 | March 1919 | | Lost 19 August 1941 |
| *Brighton* (I-08) | *Cowell* | Fore River | November 1918 | March 1919 | | Broken up 1949 |
| *Charlestown* (I-21) | *Abbot* | Newport | July 1918 | July 1919 | September 1940 | Broken up 1947 |
| *Georgetown* (I-40) | *Maddox* | Fore River | October 1918 | March 1919 | | Broken up 1952 |
| *Hamilton* (I-24) | *Kalk* | Fore River | December 1918 | March 1919 | | To Canada June 1941 |
| *Newark* (G-08) | *Ringgold* | Union | April 1918 | November 1918 | | Broken up 1947 |
| *Newmarket* (G-47) | *Robinson* | Union | March 1918 | October 1918 | December 1940 | Broken up 1945 |
| *Newport* (G-54) | *Sigourney* | Fore River | December 1917 | May 1918 | | Broken up 1947 |
| *Roxburgh* (I-07) | *Foote* | Fore River | December 1918 | March 1919 | | Broken up 1949 |
| *St Albans* (I-15) | *Thomas* | Newport | July 1918 | April 1919 | September 1940 | Broken up 1949 |
| *St Marys* (I-12) | *Doran/ Bagley* | Newport | October 1918 | August 1919 | | Broken up 1945 |

Fore River: Bethlehem Fore River Shipyard, Weymouth Fore River, MA
Union: Union Iron Works, San Francisco, CA
Newport: Newport News Shipbuilding, Newport News, VA

A depth charge detonates astern of a wartime destroyer. The British Mark VII depth charge was a 439lb steel container, containing 290lb of high explosive. It could be set to detonate at a pre-set depth of between 50ft and 400ft, and had a lethal blast radius of 20–25yds.

**Town class (Group 4 – *Belmont*) – formerly US Clemson class – 7 ships in group**

| HMS (Pennant No.) | US Navy Name | Builder | Launched | Commissioned (US Navy) | Commissioned (Royal Navy) | Fate |
|---|---|---|---|---|---|---|
| *Belmont* (H-46) | *Satterlee* | | December 1918 | December 1919 | | Lost 31 January 1942 |
| *Beverley* (H-64) | *Branch* | | April 1919 | April 1920 | | Lost 10 April 1943 |
| *Broadwater* (H-81) | *Mason* | Newport | March 1919 | February 1920 | | Lost 18 October 1942 |
| *Broadway* (H-90) | *Hunt* | | February 1920 | June 1920 | | Broken up 1947 |
| *Chesterfield* (I-28) | *Welborn C. Wood* | | March 1920 | June 1920 | October 1940 | Broken up 1947 |
| *Churchill* (I-45) | *Herndon* | Newport | May 1919 | April 1920 | | To Soviet Union, July 1944 |
| *Clare* (I-14) | *Abel P. Upshur* | | February 1920 | May 1920 | | Broken up 1945 |

Quincy: Victory Plant Shipyard, Quincy, MA
Squantum: Victory Destroyer Plant, Squantum, Quincy, MA

**Town class (Group 5 – *Bradford*) – formerly US Clemson class – 11 ships in group**

| HMS (Pennant No.) | US Navy Name | Builder | Launched | Commissioned (US Navy) | Commissioned (Royal Navy) | Fate |
|---|---|---|---|---|---|---|
| *Bradford* (H-72) | *McLanahan* | Squantum | September 1918 | April 1919 | | Broken up 1946 |
| *Burnham* (H-82) | *Aulick* | Quincy | April 1919 | July 1919 | October 1940 | Broken up 1947 |
| *Burwell* (H-94) | *Lamb* | Squantum | August 1918 | March 1919 | | Broken up 1947 |
| *Buxton* (H-96) | *Edwards* | | October 1918 | April 1919 | | Broken up 1946 |
| *Cameron* (I-05) | *Welles* | Quincy | May 1919 | September 1919 | September 1940 | Lost 5 December 1940 |
| *Ramsey* (G-60) | *Meade* | | May 1919 | September 1919 | | Broken up 1947 |
| *Reading* (G-71) | *Bailey* | | February 1919 | June 1919 | | Broken up 1945 |
| *Ripley* (G-79) | *Shubrick* | Squantum | December 1918 | July 1919 | November 1940 | Broken up 1945 |
| *Rockingham* (G-58) | *Swasey* | | May 1919 | July 1919 | | Lost 27 September 1944 |
| *Sherwood* (I-80) | *Rodgers* | | April 1919 | July 1919 | | Broken up 1945 |
| *Stanley* (I-73) | *McCalla* | Quincy | March 1919 | May 1919 | October 1940 | Lost 18 December 1941 |

The Town-class destroyer HMS *Roxburgh*, a Third (*Bath*) Group ship, pictured in mid-1943. That January she had been battered by an Atlantic storm, which had wrecked her bridge, killing her Captain and ten of her crew. She was repaired in Charleston, and resumed her deployment with the Western Local Escort Force.

HMS *Broadway* (H-90), a Fourth (*Belmont*) Group destroyer, served with the Western Approaches Command for much of the war, but in late 1943 she was converted into an Air Target Ship – a fate shared by several of the less mechanically reliable Towns. She was then stationed on the North Sea coast, where bomber crews used her for target practice.

This photograph of HMS *Ramsey* (G-60), a Town of the Fifth (*Bradford*) Group, was taken in June 1942, after she underwent her Stage 2 modifications in Boston, Massachusetts. It clearly shows her new Type 271 surface search radar in its characteristic 'Chinese lantern' dome abaft her bridge, but from the previous April she carried a Type 286 air warning radar at her masthead.

# Frigates (US Destroyer Escorts)

| Captain class (Diesel Electric group) – formerly US Evarts (or 'GMT') class – 32 ships in group | | | | |
|---|---|---|---|---|
| **Note: All but one were built in the Boston Navy Yard, Boston, MA** | | | | |
| HMS (Pennant No.) | US Navy Name | Launched | Commissioned (Royal Navy) | Fate |
| *Bayntun* (K-310) | DE-1 | June 1942 | January 1943 | Returned 1945 |
| *Bazely* .(K-311) | DE-2 | | February 1943 | |
| *Berry* (K-312) | DE-3 | November 1942 | March 1943 | Returned 1946 |
| *Blackwood* (K-313) | DE-4 | | | Lost 15 June 1944 |
| *Burges* (K-349) | DE-12 | January 1943 | June 1943 | Returned 1946 |
| *Drury** (K-316) | DE-46 | July 1942 | April 1943 | Returned 1945 |
| *Capel* (K-470) | DE-266 | April 1943 | August 1943 | Returned 1946 |
| *Cooke* (K-471) | DE-267 | | | |
| *Dacres* (K-472) | DE-268 | | | |
| *Domett* (K-473) | DE-269 | May 1943 | September 1943 | Returned 1945 |
| *Foley* (K-474) | DE-270 | | | |
| *Garlies* (K-475) | DE-271 | | | |
| *Gould* (K-476) | DE-272 | June 1943 | | Lost 1 March 1944 |
| *Grindall* (K-477) | DE-273 | June 1943 | September 1943 | Returned 1945 |
| *Gardiner* (K-478) | DE-274 | | | Returned 1946 |
| *Goodall* (K-479) | DE-275 | July 1943 | October 1943 | Lost 29 April 1945 |
| *Goodson* (K-480) | DE-276 | | | Lost 25 June 1944 |
| *Gore* (K-481) | DE-277 | | | Returned 1946 |
| *Keats* (K-482) | DE-278 | | | |
| *Kempthorne* (K-483) | DE-279 | | | Returned 1945 |
| *Kingsmill* (K-484) | DE-280 | | | |
| *Lawford* (K-514) | DE-516 | August 1943 | November 1943 | Lost 8 June 1944 |
| *Luis* (K-515) | DE-517 | | | Returned 1946 |
| *Lawson* (K-516) | DE-518 | | | |
| *Paisley* (K-564) | DE-519 | | | Returned 1945 |
| *Loring* (K-565) | DE-520 | | | Returned 1947 |
| *Hoste* (K-566) | DE-521 | September 1943 | December 1943 | Returned 1945 |
| *Moorsom* (K-567) | DE-522 | | | |
| *Manners* (K-568) | DE-523 | | | Lost 26 January 1945 |
| *Mounsey* (K-569) | DE-524 | September 1943 | December 1943 | Returned 1946 |
| *Inglis* (K-570) | DE-525 | November 1943 | | |
| *Inman* (K-571) | DE-526 | | January 1944 | |

\* HMS *Drury* was built in the Philadelphia Navy Yard, Philadelphia, PA

For much of the war HMS *Brighton* (I-57) a Third (*Bath*) Group destroyer, was attached to the 1st Minelaying Squadron, based in Kyle of Lochalsh in the west of Scotland. Her job was to protect minelayers operating as far afield as Iceland. This shows her lying off the Scottish coast during the summer of 1942. At the end of the year she was converted into an Air Target Ship.

**Captain class (Turbo-Electric group) – formerly US Buckley (or 'TE') class – 46 ships in group**
**(All built in the Bethlehem Hingham Shipyard, Hingham, MA)**

| HMS (Pennant No.) | US Navy Name | Launched | Commissioned (Royal Navy) | Fate |
|---|---|---|---|---|
| Bentinck (K-314) | DE-52 | August 1942 | May 1943 | Returned 1946 |
| Byard (K-315) | DE-55 | March 1943 | June 1943 | |
| Calder (K-349) | DE-58 | | July 1943 | Returned 1945 |
| Duckworth (K-351) | DE-61 | May 1943 | August 1943 | |
| Duff (K-352) | DE-64 | | | Lost 30 November 1944 |
| Essington (K-353) | DE-67 | June 1943 | | Returned 1945 |
| Affleck (K-462) | DE-71 | | September 1943 | Lost 26 December 1944 |
| Aylmer (K-463) | DE-72 | July 1943 | | Returned 1945 |
| Balfour (K-464) | DE-73 | | October 1943 | |
| Bentley (K-465) | DE-74 | | October 1943 | Returned 1945 |
| Bickerton (K-466) | DE-75 | July 1943 | | Lost 22 August 1944 |
| Bligh (K-467) | DE-76 | | | Returned 1945 |
| Braithwaite (K-468) | DE-77 | | November 1943 | |
| Bullen (K-460) | DE-78 | | October 1943 | Lost 6 December 1944 |
| Byron (K-508) | DE-79 | | October 1943 | |
| Conn (K-509) | DE-80 | August 1943 | | Returned 1945 |
| Cotton (K-510) | DE-81 | | | |
| Cranstoun (K-511) | DE-82 | | | |
| Cubitt (K-512) | DE-83 | | November 1943 | Returned 1946 |
| Curzon (K-513) | DE-84 | September 1943 | | |
| Dakins (K-550) | DE-85 | | | Lost 25 December 1944 |
| Deane (K-551) | DE-86 | | | Returned 1946 |
| Ekins (K-552) | DE-87 | October 1943 | | Lost 27 April 1945 |
| Fitzroy (K-553) | DE-88 | September 1943 | October 1943 | Returned 1946 |
| Redmill (K-554) | DE-89 | | November 1943 | Lost 27 April 1945 |
| Retalick (K-555) | DE-90 | | December 1943 | Returned 1945 |
| Halsted (K-556) | DE-91 | | November 1943 | Lost 10 June 1944 |
| Riou (K-557) | DE-92 | | | Returned 1946 |
| Rutherford (K-558) | DE-93 | October 1943 | | Returned 1945 |
| Cosby (K-559) | DE-94 | | | Returned 1946 |
| Rowley (K-560) | DE-95 | | December 1943 | Returned 1945 |
| Rupert (K-561) | DE-96 | | | |
| Stockham (K-562) | DE-97 | | | Returned 1946 |
| Seymour (K-563) | DE-98 | November 1943 | | |
| Spragge (K-572) | DE-563 | October 1943 | January 1944 | |
| Stayner (K-573) | DE-564 | | December 1943 | Returned 1945 |
| Thornborough (K-574) | DE-565 | | | Returned 1947 |
| Trollope (K-575) | DE-566 | November 1943 | | Lost 6 July 1944 |
| Tyler (K-576) | DE-567 | | January 1944 | Returned 1945 |
| Torrington (K-577) | DE-568 | | | Returned 1946 |
| Narborough (K-578) | DE-569 | November 1943 | | Returned 1946 |
| Waldegrave (K-579) | DE-570 | December 1943 | January 1944 | Returned 1945 |
| Whittaker (K-580) | DE-571 | | | Lost 1 November 1944 |
| Holmes (K-581) | DE-572 | | | Returned 1945 |
| Hargood (K-582) | DE-573 | December 1943 | | Returned 1946 |
| Hotham (K-583) | DE-574 | | February 1944 | Returned 1956 |

# SPECIFICATIONS

## Destroyers

| US Navy Caldwell class – became Royal Navy Town class (*Lewes* group) | |
|---|---|
| Built | 1916–20 |
| Ships in class | 6 |
| Number transferred through Lend-Lease | 3 |
| Displacement | 1,120 tons (standard); 1,187 tons (fully laden) |
| Dimensions | Length 315.6ft (96.2m) overall; Beam 30.5ft (9.3m); Draught 8.9ft (2.7m) |
| Propulsion | Two shafts, two Parsons geared turbines (Curtis turbines in *Caldwell*),* four Thornycroft boilers, generating 18,500shp |
| Maximum speed | 30 knots |
| Endurance | 2,500nm at 20 knots |
| Armament | Four 4in/50 (10.2cm) guns on single mounts, two 3in/23 (7.6cm) AA guns on single mounts, 12 21in (53.3cm) torpedoes in four triple mounts, one Y-gun depth charge projector |
| Complement | 100 |
| Lend-Lease transfers | (3) USS *Conway* (DD-70), USS *Conner* (DD-72), USS *Stockton* (DD-73) |

\* *Conner* and *Stockton* had three shafts and three geared turbines plus a cruising turbine

HMS *Churchill* (I-45), a Fourth (*Belmont*) Group destroyer of the Town class. In this picture, taken in 1942, she sports a striking camouflage pattern of light and dark grey, designed by Peter Scott. At the time she was operating in the western Atlantic, as part of the 5th Escort Group.

### US Navy Wickes class – became Royal Navy Town class (*Bath & Campbeltown* groups)

| | |
|---|---|
| Built | 1917–19 |
| Ships in class | 111 |
| Number transferred through Lend-Lease | 26 |
| Displacement | 1,090 tons (standard); 1,247 tons (fully laden) |
| Dimensions | Length 314.3ft (95.8m) overall; Beam 30.8ft (9.4m); Draught 9.2ft (2.8m) |
| Propulsion | Two shafts, two Parsons geared turbines with additional cruising turbine on port shaft, four White-Forster boilers, generating 24,200shp |
| Maximum speed | 35 knots |
| Endurance | 2,500nm at 20 knots |
| Armament | Four 4in/50 (10.2cm) guns on single mounts, one 3in/23 (7.6cm) AA gun on single mount, 12 21in (53.3cm) torpedoes in four triple mounts, one Y-gun depth charge projector |
| Complement | 114 |
| Lend-Lease transfer | (26) USS *Wickes* (DD-75), USS *Philip* (DD-76), USS *Evans* (DD-78), USS *Sigourney* (DD-81), USS *Robinson* (DD-88), USS *Ringgold* (DD-89), USS *Fairfax* (DD-93), USS *Twiggs* (DD-127), USS *Buchanan* (DD-131), USS *Aaron Ward* (DD-132), USS *Hale* (DD-133), USS *Crowninshield* (DD-134), USS *Tillman* (DD-135), USS *Claxton* (DD-140), USS *Yarnall* (DD-143), USS *Thatcher* (DD-162), USS *Cowell* (DD-167), USS *Maddox* (DD-168), USS *Foote* (DD-169), USS *Kalk* (DD-170), USS *Mackenzie* (DD-175), USS *Hopewell* (DD-181), USS *Thomas* (DD-182), USS *Haraden* (DD-183), USS *Abbot* (DD-184), USS *Bagley* – renamed *Doran* in December 1939 (DD-185). Of these, *Thatcher, Mackenzie* and *Haraden* were transferred to the Royal Canadian Navy, while the remaining destroyers were lent to the Royal Navy. |

While a third of American-built Evarts and Buckley-class destroyer escorts were commissioned into the Royal Navy, the remainder were earmarked for the US Navy. This is one of them, the Buckley-class warship USS *Liddle*. Her layout though, mirrored her British sister ships. This photo gives a good impression of the deck layout of a British Captain class frigate, with the circular mountings for her 3in guns and 20mm Oerlikons clearly visible.

### US Navy Clemson class – became Royal Navy Town class (*Belmont & Bradford* groups)

| | |
|---|---|
| Built | 1918–22 |
| Ships in class | 156 |
| Number transferred through Lend-Lease | 20 |
| Displacement | 1,190 tons (standard); 1,308 tons (fully laden) |
| Dimensions | Length: 314.3ft (95.8m) overall; Beam: 30.8ft (9.4m); Draught: 9.8ft (3m) |
| Propulsion | Two shafts, two Westinghouse geared turbines, four White-Forster boilers, generating 27,000shp |
| Maximum speed | 35 knots |
| Endurance | 2,500 nm at 20 knots |
| Armament | Four 4in/50 (10.2cm) guns on single mounts, one 3in/23 (7.6cm) AA gun on single mount, 12 21in (53.3cm) torpedoes in four triple mounts, one Y-gun depth charge projector |
| Complement | 114 |

Lend-Lease transfers (20) USS *Satterlee* (DD-190), USS *Mason* (DD-191), USS *Abel P. Upshur* (DD-193), USS *Hunt* (DD-194), USS *Welborn C. Wood* (DD-195), USS *Branch* (DD-197), USS *Herndon* (DD-198), USS *McCook* (DD-252), USS *McCalla* (DD-253), USS *Rodgers* (DD-254), USS *Bancroft* (DD-256), USS *Aulick* (DD-258), USS *Welles* (DD-257), USS *Lamb* (DD-263), USS *McLanahan* (DD-264), USS *Edwards* (DD-265), USS *Shubrick* (DD-268), USS *Bailey* (DD-269), USS *Swasey* (DD-273), USS *Meade* (DD-274). Of these, *McCook* and *Bancroft* were transferred to the Royal Canadian Navy, while the remaining destroyers were lent to the Royal Navy.

# Frigates (US Destroyer Escorts)

## US Navy Evarts (or GMT) class – became Royal Navy Captain class (GMT group)

| | |
|---|---|
| Built | 1942–45 |
| Ships in class | 97 |
| Number transferred through Lend-Lease | 32 |
| Displacement | 1,192 tons (standard); 1,416 tons (fully laden) |
| Dimensions | Length: 289.4ft (88.2m) overall; Beam: 35.1ft (10.7m); Draught: 10.2ft (3.1m) |
| Propulsion | Two shafts, two General Electric diesel engines, generating 6,000bhp |
| Maximum speed | 19.5 knots |
| Endurance | 6,000nm at 12 knots |
| Armament | Three 3in/50 (7.6cm) guns on single mounts, four 1.1in AA guns in quadruple mount, nine 20mm guns in single mounts, two 21in (53.3cm) torpedoes in triple mount, one Hedgehog, eight depth charge throwers, two depth charge racks |
| Complement | 156 |
| Lend-Lease transfers | (32): DE-1–4, DE-12, DE-46, DE-266–280, DE-516–526 |

*Note*: These ships were never commissioned into the US Navy

## US Navy Buckley (or TE) class – became Royal Navy Captain class (TE group)

| | |
|---|---|
| Built | 1942–46 |
| Ships in class | 102 |
| Number transferred through Lend-Lease | 46 |
| Displacement | 1,432 tons (standard); 1,823 tons (fully laden) |
| Dimensions | Length: 306.1ft (93.3m) overall; Beam: 37.1ft (11.3m); Draught: 11.2ft (3.4m) |
| Propulsion | Two shafts, two General Electric turbines, two boilers, generating 12,000shp |
| Maximum speed | 23 knots |
| Endurance | 6,000nm at 12 knots |
| Armament | Three 3in/50 (7.6cm) guns on single mounts, four 1.1in AA guns in quadruple mount, eight 20mm guns in single mounts, two 21in (53.3cm) torpedoes in triple mount, one Hedgehog, eight depth charge throwers, two depth charge racks |
| Complement | 186 |
| Lend-Lease transfers (46) | DE-52, DE-55, DE-58, DE-61, DE-64, DE-67, DE-71–98, DE-563–574 |

*Note*: These ships were never commissioned into the US Navy.

# FURTHER READING

Brown, David K., *Atlantic Escorts: Ships Weapons and Tactics in World War II* (Barnsley: Seaforth Publishing, 2022)

Brown, Les, *British Sloops and Frigates of the Second World War*, Shipcraft Series, no. 27 (Barnsley: Seaforth Publishing, 2021)

Brown, Les, *British Escort Destroyers of the Second World War*, Shipcraft Series, no. 28 (Barnsley: Seaforth Publishing, 2022)

Campbell, John, *Naval Weapons of World War Two* (London: Conway Maritime Press, 1985)

Collingwood, Donald, *The Captain Class Frigates in the Second World War* (Barnsley: Leo Cooper, 1999)

Friedman, Norman, *Naval Radar* (London: Conway Maritime Press, 1981)

Friedman, Norman, *British Destroyers: The Second World War and After* (Barnsley: Seaforth Publishing, 2006)

Gardiner, Robert (ed.), *Conway's All the World's Fighting Warships, 1922–1946* (London: Conway Maritime Press, 1980)

Goodhart, Philip, *Fifty Ships that Saved the World* (London: William Heinemann Ltd, 1965)

Henry, Chris, *Depth Charge: Royal Naval Mines, Depth Charges & Underwater Weapons, 1914–1945* (Barnsley: Pen & Sword, 2005)

Henshaw, John, *Town Class Destroyers: A Critical Assessment* (Marlborough: Crowood Press, 2018)

Hodges, Peter and Friedman, Norman, *Destroyer Weapons of World War 2* (London: HarperCollins, 1979)

Konstam, Angus, *The Convoy: HG-76 – Taking the Fight to Hitler's U-boats* (Oxford: Osprey Publishing, 2023)

Lavery, Brian, *Churchill's Navy: The Ships, Men and Organization, 1939–45* (London: Conway Maritime Press, 2006)

Lenton, Henry Trevor, *British Fleet and Escort Destroyers,* vols 1 and 2, Navies of the Second World War Series (London: Macdonald, 1970)

Manning, T.D., *The British Destroyer* (London: Putnam, 1961)

Preston, Antony (ed.), *Jane's Fighting Ships of World War II* (London: Bracken Books, 1989)

Raven, Alan, *Camouflage, Royal Navy*, Warships in Perspective Series, 3 vols (New York, NY: W.R. Press, 2000-01)

Roberts, John, *British Warships of the Second World War*, Blueprints Series (London: Chatham Publishing, 2000) Revised and republished in 2017 by Seaforth Publishing

Whitley, M.J., *Destroyers of World War Two* (London: Cassell, 1988)

Wright, Malcolm, *British and Commonwealth Warship Camouflage of WWII*, vol. 1 (Barnsley: Seaforth Publishing, 2014)

# INDEX